Decisions, Decisions

DEVOTIONS FOR KIDS

Decisions, Decisions

DEVOTIONS FOR KIDS

TRISHA WHITE PRIEBE

BARBOUR **kidz**

A Division of Barbour Publishing

Published in Association with Jessica Kirkland and the literary agency of Kirkland Media Management, LLC. P.O. Box 1539, Liberty, Texas 77575.

Published by Barbour Publishing, Inc., 1810 Barbour Drive, Uhrichsville, Ohio 44683, www.barbourbooks.com

Our mission is to inspire the world with the life-changing message of the Bible.

Member of the
Evangelical Christian
Publishers Association

Printed in the United States of America.

000738 0421 BP

For Calvin, Stanley, and Claire. You aren't mine, but I sure love you like you are. I can't wait to see what choices you make, and how God uses your decisions—big and small—to guide your future. I'll be the crazy aunt cheering from the sidelines.

CONTENTS

DECISIONS, DECISIONS. . .

The new kid at school looks lonely. . .should you go over and say hi?

Mom told you to clean your room. . .but wouldn't you rather join your friends at the park?

You just found a wallet full of money. . .is it time to buy that new device you've been wanting?

. . .WHAT WILL YOU DO?

We make decisions every day. Some are small and unimportant, like which pair of socks we'll wear. Others are much bigger, like the decisions you'd make in the examples above.

This book is all about choices. Here are forty short stories that describe real-life situations any kid could face, at home, at school, at church, or on the playing field. Each story features a decision point, that moment when the character needs to choose what to do. Put yourself in the character's shoes, and decide how he or she should respond!

There are three possible options with each story, and some choices are better than others. (Some choices just stink, really.) The best ones are the ones that align with the Bible's teaching and honor God.

And that's the most important message of this book—you'll have a much happier and more satisfying life when you make *godly* decisions. You've already made a great choice to start reading this book. . .keep reading to see how your good decisions can make you and your world better.

One

JUST A TEST

Olivia slid into her desk at school right as the morning bell rang.

It had been a long weekend of babysitting her little brother while her parents cared for her sick grandmother, and Olivia was tired. She could barely keep her eyes open. All she wanted to do was finish the school day and go home.

Actually, what she really wanted was for Friday to come fast!

Olivia was excited because she had worked hard over the previous few weeks to raise her grades, and this Friday she would be able to attend her school's homecoming basketball game—the biggest game of the year—with her friends. All she needed to do was keep her eyes on the prize and not make any big mistakes or forget any important assignments.

What could go wrong?

Then her teacher, Mrs. Wilson, smiled at the class and said the worst possible thing: "Students, clear your desks. It's time to take your math test."

Math test! Olivia's heart began to race, and her eyes

filled with tears. With such a busy weekend of helping her parents, she had completely forgotten about the math test. She knew there was no way she would do well enough to keep her grade at the level that would allow her to attend the basketball game.

As Mrs. Wilson began passing out the test, Olivia noticed that she was sitting in the perfect spot to see directly onto a classmate's paper. Andrew was really good at math, and Olivia knew if she copied just a few of his answers, she could probably do well enough to go to the game. Plus, she wouldn't disappoint her parents with a bad test grade.

If you were Olivia, what would you do?

Decision 1: Copy some of Andrew's answers, just this once. (turn to page 13)
Decision 2: Take the test, knowing you would probably not go to the game. (turn to page 14)
Decision 3: Raise your hand and ask to talk to Mrs. Wilson in the hallway. (turn to page 15)

DECISION 1:

Olivia didn't feel good about copying Andrew's answers, but she wanted so badly to go to the basketball game. When Mrs. Wilson stopped at another student's desk to answer a question, Olivia looked at Andrew's paper. She carefully copied his answers onto her page. As she was writing, Olivia felt someone tap her on the shoulder. She turned to see Jack, the student behind her, who said, "I see what you're doing, and I'm going to tell." Olivia's heart sank. She felt even worse about what she had done than she felt about forgetting the test. She wished she had just been honest.

DECISION 2:

The tears clouding her eyes made it hard to see her paper, but Olivia knew it would be wrong to steal Andrew's answers. She looked at the first question, but all she could think about was how sad she would be to miss the game—and how upset her parents would be that she forgot to study for the test. Finally, with too much on her mind to think clearly, she just gave up and started writing numbers in the answer spaces. *They're probably all wrong,* she thought, *but what difference does it make?*

DECISION 3:

Olivia looked down at her test, unable to remember how to even start the first math problem. Her stomach hurt, and she wanted to cry. She closed her eyes and prayed silently, *Lord, I need Your help.* When she opened her eyes, Mrs. Wilson was standing beside her desk. "Is everything okay, Olivia?" Olivia shook her head. She stood from her desk and walked with Mrs. Wilson into the hallway, where Olivia described the long weekend of caring for her brother and how her grandmother was sick. Mrs. Wilson explained that she couldn't always provide exceptions, but that this once, she would give Olivia one more day to study for the test.

WHY DOES IT MATTER?

Cheating on a test may not feel like a big deal. It doesn't seem like it hurts anyone, and it can actually feel helpful at the time. But cheating is lying and stealing—and God hates both. Proverbs 12:22 says, "The Lord hates lying lips, but those who speak the truth are His joy." Many times the Bible warns against taking other people's things—"Do not steal" is even one of the Ten Commandments (Exodus 20:15). As hard as it can be to tell the truth in a tough situation (like taking a test we didn't study for), God gives us everything we need to pass *His* test (like telling the truth) with flying colors. Let's always seek to do what pleases Him.

TWO

A LESSON FROM THE ANTS

Griffin dropped his book bag by the front door and flopped onto the couch.

It was still August, and he was already tired of going to school. All he really wanted to do was take naps, eat snacks, and play video games. *Wouldn't that be an amazing life?*

Tucking his hands behind his head and looking up to the ceiling, Griffin said to himself, "When I grow up, I'm not going to do *anything*."

He closed his eyes, imagining a life with no responsibility, when his stomach growled. "Mom!" he called, but there was no answer. "Mom!" he called even louder, but still there was only silence.

He sighed loudly, pushed himself up from the couch, and dragged his feet to the kitchen in search of something to eat. Pulling open the cupboard, he was horrified by what he discovered.

There—where he had dropped a spoonful of jelly before school—was a long trail of busy ants. Scurrying along the same careful path, each ant gathered some of the jelly and then turned and followed a second path back out of the cupboard.

Griffin followed the trail of ants to the back door and out onto the porch.

He remembered his teacher saying that ants are some of the hardest-working creatures in nature. They work hard to keep their colony clean—lifting twenty times their own body weight—and they work hard to meet each other's needs.

"I'm glad I'm not an ant!" Griffin said.

He went back inside the house and discovered a note from his mom on the counter. "Dear Griffin," he read out loud. "I'm running errands and won't be home for a couple of hours. Make good choices."

He set the note down. With nobody home to tell him what to do, he could do whatever he wanted.

If you were Griffin, what would you do?

Decision 1: Relax. It's been a long day, and there will always be time later to get things done. (turn to page 19)
Decision 2: Start on homework while watching television. (turn to page 20)
Decision 3: Clean up the jelly mess and then start on your homework. (turn to page 21)

DECISION 1:

Griffin had spent an entire day at school with a teacher who expected him to work hard, so he believed he deserved to relax. He kicked off his shoes, turned on his console, and got lost in his favorite video game. All he wanted to do was beat the next level, and then he would start on his homework. But next thing he knew, two hours had passed—and his mom was pulling into the driveway! Griffin hadn't made a single good decision since he got home from school, and now his mom would be disappointed in him.

DECISION 2:

Griffin turned on the television and began flipping through the channels. Nothing he wanted to watch was on, but he really didn't want to do his homework. So he watched a few cartoons and stared at the weather channel while halfheartedly completing a few of the sentences for his English assignment. Pretty soon Griffin heard his mom's car pull into the driveway, and he looked down at the paper on his lap. His work was sloppy, and he hadn't completed much. He hadn't really enjoyed his time watching TV, and now he'd have to spend the rest of the evening doing work. He knew he should have just done his homework first so he could enjoy some time relaxing.

DECISION 3:

Griffin thought about the ants and how hard they work. He decided if they could work hard, so could he. First, he cleaned up the jelly he'd spilled that morning. After all, why should his mom be expected to clean up his mess? Next, he took out his English book and began working on his homework assignment. It wasn't his favorite thing, but he knew if he got it done, he would be able to spend his evening doing the stuff he loved. Maybe he could even convince his mom to play a game with him when she got home.

WHY DOES IT MATTER?

God wants us to work hard. In fact, He tells us in Proverbs, "Go to the ant, O lazy person. Watch and think about her ways, and be wise. She has no leader, head or ruler, but she gets her food ready in the summer, and gathers her food at the right time" (Proverbs 6:6–8). If the ant—who can't know or worship God—works hard, we as people should be able to work even harder because we work for the Lord. All of our work—whether we're cleaning up jelly spills, doing our homework, or going to a job someday—should be done to please God.

THREE

ALL ABOUT CHANGE

After a long morning of Saturday chores, Ava and her best friend, Sophia, stood in their favorite ice cream shop. It was a good day, and it was about to get even better. Main Street Scoops made the best ice cream *anywhere*.

Ava could already taste the delicious treat, and she hadn't even ordered yet!

It took Ava a long time to earn money, and she felt a little sad spending most of it at once—but she really wanted some vanilla ice cream with hot fudge sauce.

She ordered her ice cream and handed the girl behind the counter four dollars, knowing she should get fifty cents back in change.

The employee wore a button that said "I'm new!" and Ava could tell she was nervous. The girl opened and closed the register a couple times and looked around like she was confused. Other workers were busy scooping ice cream for other customers, so the new employee was left to figure things out on her own.

Finally, the girl handed Ava two dollars in change—*a dollar and fifty cents too much.*

Ava opened her mouth to tell the girl that she had given back too much money, but then she stopped. It wasn't Ava's fault that the girl didn't give her the right amount of money. And anyway, would a business as big as Main Street Scoops really miss a dollar and fifty cents? Surely they made hundreds of dollars every day.

It would be nice to have a little money left over, wouldn't it?

If you were Ava, what would you do?

Decision 1: Kindly tell the new girl that she had given too much change and return a dollar and fifty cents. (turn to page 25)

Decision 2: Keep the change for next time, knowing you'd probably spend it at Main Street Scoops anyway. (turn to page 26)

Decision 3: Do something good with the extra money, like give it to someone in need. (turn to page 27)

DECISION 1:

"Excuse me," Ava said to the new girl behind the counter. "You accidentally gave me too much change." Ava held out the two dollars and explained that she should only have received fifty cents. The employee looked very relieved and quickly corrected her error. She thanked Ava for telling the truth, and Ava had the chance to explain that her relationship with Jesus was more important to her than anything. She then invited the new girl to come with her to church. On her way home, Ava realized she was happier with only fifty cents in her pocket and a clean conscience.

DECISION 2:

Ava put the two dollars in her pocket and left Main Street Scoops with Sophia. Together, they licked their ice cream as they walked home, but it was the strangest thing—Ava's ice cream didn't taste nearly as good as it usually did. Instead of enjoying her favorite treat, all she could think about was the money in her pocket and how she should have told the new girl about her mistake. Ava learned that *integrity* (a word that means being honest no matter what) is better than getting an extra dollar and fifty cents.

DECISION 3:

Ava wished she hadn't taken the extra money. Her conscience—that little voice inside that told her when she was doing something wrong—wouldn't be quiet long enough for her to enjoy her ice cream. She knew she should go back to Main Street Scoops. But then she saw a man sitting on the street corner with a sign asking for money. Eagerly, she approached the man and handed him the two dollars in her pocket. But it was weird: even though she gave him the extra money—as well as fifty cents of her own—she still had a sinking feeling in her stomach that wouldn't go away.

WHY DOES IT MATTER?

Any time we take or keep something that doesn't belong to us—money, toys, clothes, or anything at all—it is stealing. The eighth of the Ten Commandments tells us not to steal. . .so we're sinning against God whenever we take or keep what doesn't belong to us. That's true even if someone else made a mistake. God's solution for stealing is to work hard and be generous. Ephesians 4:28 tells us, "Anyone who steals must stop it! He must work with his hands so he will have what he needs and can give to those who need help." We must have the courage to be honest and refuse to take what isn't ours.

FOUR

GOD OF THE TORNADOES

The loud sound pierced the air, and Noah sat up in his bed. He knew the sound of a tornado siren anywhere— he and his family had lived through a tornado when he was just three years old. Its wind had completely destroyed their home, and that was the reason they had ended up moving to another town.

It still made Noah sad to think about the friends he had left behind.

Now heavy rain pelted his bedroom windows, and the sound of thunder boomed in the distance while the siren continued to wail. Noah wondered if his family would lose everything again and move to yet another city. The problem was that he liked where they were living, and he didn't want to go.

Suddenly, the hall lights came on, and Noah's parents appeared in his doorway. His dad said, "Let's go downstairs where we'll be safer." But Noah couldn't move. His heart pounded and his legs felt numb from the fear. "Come on!" his dad shouted, but Noah still sat in his bed.

"I don't want to go," Noah finally said, but he wasn't

talking about going downstairs.

He didn't want to move to a new house or city.

Noah's dad walked to his bed and gently scooped him up.

Even though Noah was almost ten years old, it felt good to be safe in his father's arms.

Once the family—including their old dog Barney—was safely downstairs, Dad asked Noah kindly, "Can you trust God?"

Noah's eyes filled with tears. He didn't know how to tell his parents that trusting God was hard when God had already allowed them to lose everything. What would stop God from doing it again? Could He really be trusted?

Noah's dad opened his Bible and read Psalm 56:3, "When I am afraid, I will trust in You."

If you were Noah, what would you do?

Decision 1: Trust God only if the storm passes and the house is not destroyed. (turn to page 31)

Decision 2: Understand that fear is a natural part of life, but God wants us to trust Him no matter what. (turn to page 32)

Decision 3: Refuse to trust God. A good God wouldn't let bad things happen. (turn to page 33)

DECISION 1:

Noah waited with his family in the basement until the storm finally passed. When everything grew quiet outside, Noah's dad went upstairs to check on the house, then he came downstairs with the good news that everything was okay.

Noah crawled back into his bed and lay awake for a long time. He decided he would trust God for now since God had protected their house from the storm. But as he drifted off to sleep, he wondered if that was truly good enough. Noah knew in his heart that he wasn't really trusting God if he only trusted when God did what he wanted.

DECISION 2:

Noah curled up under his father's arm and thought about how safe he felt knowing his dad loved and protected him. He thought about a verse he had learned in Sunday school. Second Corinthians 6:18 says, "I will be a Father to you. You will be My sons and daughters, says the All-powerful God."

Noah knew that God had promised to be a Father to anyone who followed Jesus. And Noah also knew that God had said He would never leave His children alone. No matter how scared Noah was, he knew he could trust God to be with him every step of the way.

Before he drifted off to sleep, Noah prayed and thanked God for being so trustworthy.

DECISION 3:

Noah loved going to church and learning about God, but he wasn't sure he was ready to trust Him with his whole life. What if more bad things happened? What if he and his family lost their house and had to move away a second time? He decided he would trust God when he was older and when fewer bad things happened.

Even as Noah had these thoughts, he realized that he only grew more afraid. He thought it would be easier *not* to trust God, but so far, not trusting God made scary moments like these even scarier. Noah felt totally alone.

WHY DOES IT MATTER?

God's love for us is so big, so deep, and so wide that it is *incomprehensible*—a word that means we can't begin to understand it, even if we try. In fact, God loves us so much that He even allows hard things into our lives sometimes, knowing they will draw us closer to Him and make us more like Christ. He wants what is best for us, even if what is best doesn't feel good. But even in the times when we're scared, He promises never to leave us. We can *always* trust Him. He is a good Father.

Five

A GOLDEN OPPORTUNITY

Emma wanted badly to be friends with a group of girls in her class at school, but they never seemed to have time for her. They didn't invite her to sit with them at lunch, and they never invited her over to their homes after school, no matter how often Emma invited them to her house.

She knew that—in order to be accepted into their group—she would need to do something to impress them.

One afternoon during recess she was given a golden opportunity.

Emma knew that the girls did not like their fellow classmate Kate. Kate came from a family that didn't have much money, so she couldn't buy the nicest clothes or afford the newest accessories. The girls were always talking about Kate and laughing at what she was wearing.

Emma thought Kate was a nice girl, but if being mean to Kate was the only way to be friends with the other girls, Emma thought it might be worth it.

During recess, Emma overheard the teacher

talking to Kate's mom, and she learned that Kate's dad had made a big mistake and was now in jail. Emma knew the group of girls would love to hear this news. If she shared it, they would definitely accept her!

She looked across the playground. In one corner, Emma saw the group of girls huddled together laughing. In the other corner, she saw Kate standing alone.

Kate was living with the heavy secret that her dad was no longer at home to love her or take care of her, so she needed a friend right now more than ever.

But this was also Emma's chance to be accepted.

Emma realized she needed to choose between the group of girls and Kate.

If you were Emma, what would you do?

Decision 1: Keep the secret to yourself and look for another way to earn the girls' approval. (turn to page 37)

Decision 2: Tell the group of girls that Kate's dad is in jail. He made the big mistake, after all, so you would just be sharing facts. (turn to page 38)

Decision 3: Recognize that these girls aren't the right kind of friends, and spend time instead with Kate, who needs a good friend in her life right now. (turn to page 39)

DECISION 1:

Emma decided she would look for another way to earn the girls' approval. Something didn't feel right about sharing the news of Kate's dad being in jail. Emma knew she wouldn't want them to know if her own dad made a big mistake, and she was sure the girls wouldn't be kind about it. It would only give them one more thing to laugh at. That made her wonder if she should even want to be their friend at all. She thought about it, wondering if being popular was better than being kind. Then she thought about how Jesus had acted when He was on earth—how He was kind to everyone, especially those who were hurting—and realized she needed to think about it some more.

DECISION 2:

Emma jumped at the opportunity and raced across the playground to the group of girls.

"I have something to tell you!" she said excitedly. The girls turned and listened as she told them Kate's secret. But the words felt awful coming out of her mouth, and she suddenly wished she hadn't said anything at all.

She could see Kate looking sad and lonely, and Emma immediately knew she had done the wrong thing.

Once Emma was finished telling Kate's secret, the group of girls turned back and continued laughing and talking without her.

Emma felt no better for being so unkind. In fact, she only felt worse.

DECISION 3:

Emma really wanted to be accepted by the group of girls in her class, but seeing Kate standing alone across the playground made Emma realize even more that Kate needed a friend.

Emma crossed the playground and stood beside Kate.

"Want to come to my house this weekend and make cookies?" Emma asked.

Kate smiled. "Really? I didn't think you wanted to be my friend."

"I do," said Emma. "Maybe we could even convince my mom to let us paint!"

Emma saw how much her kindness had cheered Kate up, so she decided never to say anything to anyone about Kate's dad. After all, treating Kate with kindness is what Jesus would have done if He were in her shoes.

WHY DOES IT MATTER?

Wanting friends is a good thing. God gave us friends to help us live our Christian life in a way that pleases Him. So whenever we meet people who want us to do or say sinful things to be accepted, we should think carefully about whether those friends are the ones we should want to have in our lives.

First Corinthians 15:33 says, "Do not let anyone fool you. Bad people can make those who want to live good become bad."

Good friends will encourage us to love Jesus and please God.

A LOST CAUSE

Lucas stood in the goal box, his heart beating so loudly in his ears that he wondered if his team could hear it too. This was the soccer championship game he had dreamed of for years, and now was the moment of truth. His team hadn't played as well as they usually did, and now this penalty kick would determine who won the game.

The fans in the school bleachers were cheering, Lucas's teammates were shouting his name, and his opponent—a student from Washington Middle School—was walking to the penalty line to set up his shot.

Lucas took a deep breath and nervously shifted his arms and legs. He never imagined that the outcome of this important game would depend on him.

He bent his knees, held out his arms, and whispered a quick prayer that God would help him stop the ball.

The referee blew her whistle, and Lucas's opponent took his kick. Like a flash of lightning, the ball flew toward the goal, and Lucas had only a fraction of a second to decide which way he would move to block it.

And he chose the wrong way.

He lunged left as the ball sailed into the right side of the net.

The fans from Washington Middle School cheered wildly while Lucas's team just stood quietly on the sidelines.

For a moment, all Lucas could do was lie on the ground, his head against the cold grass. Not only would his dream of winning this championship never come true, but he would also live with the knowledge that it was his own fault.

He had let his team down.

If you were Lucas, what would you do?

Decision 1: Blame the team for not playing a better game and avoiding a shoot-out. (turn to page 43)

Decision 2: Stand up, brush it off, and act like it doesn't really matter. (turn to page 44)

Decision 3: Acknowledge that losing hurts but stand up anyway and shake hands with the winning team. (turn to page 45)

DECISION 1:

Lucas punched the ground. If his teammates had played the way they should have played, a shoot-out wouldn't have been necessary! He pushed himself up and stomped off the field to where his team was waiting. He would give them a piece of his mind and let them know exactly whose fault it was.

What Lucas didn't remember was that some of his teammates as well as some of the fans in the crowd knew that he was a Christian, and that they were all watching to see how he responded. By losing his temper, Lucas was telling everyone what mattered to him most.

DECISION 2:

Lucas's stomach hurt and his heart pounded. He wanted to cry or hide—or both. But he knew he shouldn't do either, so he stuffed his feelings deep inside.

He pushed himself up from the ground, dusted off his knees, and grinned. His teammates ran to meet him in the goal box and tell him how proud they were of him for trying his best.

"Are you okay?" his teammate Carter asked.

"I'm fine," Lucas said, plastering a fake smile on his face. "It doesn't even bother me that we lost. It's just a game."

DECISION 3:

With his face on the ground and the cheering from the Washington Middle School fans getting louder, Lucas closed his eyes and prayed. "God, You know I did my best. You also know how sad I am that I couldn't win this game for my team. Please give me the courage I need to have the right attitude."

When he opened his eyes, he saw his teammates gathered around him.

Jacob held out a hand, and Lucas took it and got to his feet.

"Good game," Lucas said, looking his teammates in the eyes. "We all did our best, but the other team did a good job too. Let's go congratulate them."

WHY DOES IT MATTER?

Winning is fun, and we should always try our best in every competition, but winning isn't *everything*. In fact, winning a game isn't even the most important thing.

Did you know you can be a winner at losing and a loser at winning? First Corinthians 10:31 tells us, "So if you eat or drink or whatever you do, do everything to honor God."

We can lose a competition, have the right attitude, and be a winner in God's eyes. However, we can also win a competition, brag to everybody about it, and be a loser in what matters the most.

The real victory belongs to those who do their best and give the glory to God, no matter the outcome.

Seven

RUNNING THE SHOW

Sofia was very excited. Tonight her parents were going out on a date, and her older brother William was spending the night with friends, so she would have the house to herself. Even better, she could choose what she wanted to watch on television.

She popped a bag of popcorn and settled onto the couch with the remote.

Her parents had given her careful instructions about the shows she could watch, and thankfully, her favorite show was on the list. She turned the television on early to the right channel, hoping she wouldn't miss a moment of her show.

But as she flipped through the channels, she started noticing other shows she had never seen before. Some of them used bad language, and others showed people doing things that the Bible called sin. At first, she didn't stop to watch but just kept changing the channel. Then—after a few minutes—she started pausing a little longer. Before long, she had stopped changing the channel and just watched.

Instead of being excited about the show she had

47

wanted to watch, she suddenly grew curious about shows that she knew her parents—as well as God—wouldn't want her to see.

She glanced at the clock, seeing that it would be hours before her parents got home from their date, so nobody would know if she watched a few shows that were off-limits.

Besides, would it really hurt to watch a show on television?

She knew the choice was up to her.

If you were Sofia, what would you do?

Decision 1: Watch whatever you want. Television isn't a big deal, and you can handle it. (turn to page 49)

Decision 2: Refuse to watch a full show that is off-limits, but instead flip through the channels and see a little bit more than your parents would allow. After all, they didn't say anything about channel surfing. (turn to page 50)

Decision 3: Watch only the shows your parents have approved, even if you don't totally agree with their decision. (turn to page 51)

DECISION 1:

Sofia started watching a show that wasn't *too* bad, but she still knew it was something her parents wouldn't want her to see. Next thing she knew, she found herself watching something a little bit worse, and by the time she heard her parents pulling into the driveway, she realized she had spent an entire evening watching things that didn't please God. In fact, she felt dirty and ashamed and knew she would have a hard time forgetting some of the things she saw. She wished she had obeyed her parents.

DECISION 2:

Sofia knew she would feel bad about watching a show that was totally off-limits, so she didn't watch one show—she watched *several*. She spent a few minutes on one channel, then a few minutes on the next channel. That way if her parents asked her, she could tell them she hadn't watched any show entirely. Strangely, this didn't make Sofia feel any better about her decision, since she knew in her heart she was deceptive by intentionally misleading her parents. Instead of having enjoyed her favorite show, she just felt miserable.

DECISION 3:

Sometimes Sofia thought her parents were a little too strict with what they let her watch on television, but she still knew that they loved her and wanted to protect her. She also understood that even if they couldn't see what choices she made while they were on their date, God could see her, and she knew God honored obedience. Even though a couple of shows caught her attention and she wanted to stop and watch, she chose instead to watch the show her parents had approved. Best of all, she knew she would have a clean conscience when her parents got home.

WHY DOES IT MATTER?

Psalm 101:3 says, "I will set no sinful thing in front of my eyes. I hate the work of those who are not faithful. It will not get hold of me."

Sometimes entertainment is good at making sinful things look enjoyable or harmless. *What movies or shows should I watch? What books or magazines should I read? What games should I play on the internet?*

The Bible was written long before people had to worry about any of these questions, but the truths in the Bible are still just as important today.

What we watch with our eyes has the power to change our minds and our hearts, so God wants us to guard what we see. . .whether anybody knows what we're watching or not.

EiGHT

THE COURAGE TO TRUST

Jack loved his grandfather very much. In fact, he was even named after his grandpa!

Often on Saturdays, Jack would go to his grandpa's house, where they would do fun projects together in Grandpa Jack's garage. They did everything from making a birdhouse and repairing an old bookshelf to building a tree fort and rebuilding an old go-cart.

Jack loved spending time with his grandpa. They talked about important things, and they made plans for the future. One day, they decided when Jack graduated from high school, they would take a trip to Germany, where Grandpa Jack had been born.

Jack could hardly wait! Sometimes at night, instead of going to sleep, he would lie awake, imagining how fun this trip would be.

Then one Saturday morning, Jack's parents walked into his room and sat on the corner of his bed as he was waking up.

"What's wrong?" Jack asked. He could tell by his parents' faces that they were about to tell him something that he didn't want to hear.

"It's Grandpa Jack," his dad said. "He didn't wake up this morning. Sometime during the night, he went to heaven to be with Jesus."

"No!" Jack yelled, pushing himself up in bed and shaking his head. "Today we're supposed to build a toolbox together!" He jumped out of bed, but his dad reached out and pulled him close. Jack began to cry as he felt anger grow inside of him.

This wasn't the first time Jack had lost someone he loved. His Grandma Joy had already gone to heaven two years earlier after being sick with cancer.

Jack knew he had to make a choice. Would he trust that God knew best and only did what was good, or would he grow bitter with God, who kept taking the people he loved?

If you were Jack, what would you do?

Decision 1: Be sad over losing someone you love, but trust that God has a good plan for your life, even during your pain. (turn to page 55)

Decision 2: Wait to see if God will earn your trust back. After all, a good God wouldn't allow hurtful situations into your life. (turn to page 56)

Decision 3: Stop trusting God. You can't go to church and worship Someone who took your grandpa to heaven. (turn to page 57)

DECISION 1:

Jack was sad, but he knew his grandpa would want him to trust God, even though it was hard. Jack prayed and asked God to help him, telling God how hard it was not to see Grandpa Jack or spend time with him. But he also thanked God for the years they had shared. Jack was surprised and comforted by a peace that he couldn't explain. It reminded him of a verse he read in Sunday school. Philippians 4:7 says, "The peace of God is much greater than the human mind can understand. This peace will keep your hearts and minds through Christ Jesus." He knew God loved him and would help him.

DECISION 2:

Jack knew he should trust God just like his grandpa had always taught him—and just like the Bible says in hundreds of different verses—but he just couldn't do it. He didn't think a good God would allow things like cancer, accidents, and pain. Jack didn't see the point of any of it. It made more sense to him that Grandpa Jack and Grandma Joy should still be here on earth with him. So Jack prayed and told God that for now he would wait to see if God really could be trusted. He hoped telling God how he really felt would make him feel better, but it didn't feel good at all. Instead of feeling relief, Jack felt sad and alone.

DECISION 3:

Jack's parents and grandparents had always told him that God loved him. In fact, they often shared Jeremiah 31:3, where God says, "I have loved you with a love that lasts forever." But if that was true, why did God allow bad things to happen? Jack decided that God was either not good, not real, or not caring. None of those things described the God that Jack wanted to love and serve with his life, so Jack told God that he would not trust Him until God sent his Grandpa Jack and Grandma Joy back. Jack had never felt worse than when he prayed those words.

WHY DOES IT MATTER?

We can't always see the point of a disappointment. But we should remember that God has His own reasons for them—and He is trying to help us grow. Second Corinthians 4:17–18 says, "The little troubles we suffer now for a short time are making us ready for the great things God is going to give us forever. We do not look at the things that can be seen. We look at the things that cannot be seen. The things that can be seen will come to an end. But the things that cannot be seen will last forever."

God can be trusted with every detail in our lives.

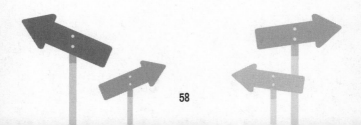

Nine

WORD TO THE WISE

Isabella was excited to be invited to the birthday party of her Sunday school friend Mia. Mia was popular and outgoing, and all her friends were accepted by the rest of the class. Isabella knew this was *her* chance to be accepted.

The day of the party arrived, and Isabella couldn't wait to go. She put on her favorite dress, fixed her hair perfectly, and wrapped Mia's gift. *I hope Mia will like the gemstone kit as much as I do.*

Isabella's mom drove her to the party, reminding her of the family's rules: *Honor God in everything you say and do. Tell the truth. Think of others. Say "thank you."*

Isabella had heard these reminders so many times, she could recite them in her sleep.

Once they arrived, Isabella hugged her mom and jumped out of the car. She raced to her friends, who were whispering and laughing in a small circle.

Isabella waved to her mom, and one of the girls laughed at her.

"Do you still wave at your mom?" the girl asked.

Isabella nodded, and the girls giggled. "Aren't you

too old for that?" another girl asked. Then she said a word Isabella was never allowed to use at home.

Another girl repeated the word, and all eyes turned to Isabella.

Isabella thought saying the word would earn her respect, but she also knew it wouldn't honor God.

What would it hurt if I use a bad word? Everyone else is saying it. Are words really a big deal?

If you were Isabella, what would you do?

Decision 1: Refuse to say the word but don't tell your friends they were wrong. What they choose to say is between them and God. (turn to page 61)

Decision 2: Say the word if it means remaining friends with them. You might have more influence as their friend. (turn to page 62)

Decision 3: Kindly encourage the girls not to say the word. (turn to page 63)

DECISION 1:

Isabella knew she shouldn't say the bad word, but she also didn't want to lose her chance at being their friend. When another girl used a bad word, Isabella just laughed and looked away. *Maybe if I change the subject, they'll stop*, she thought.

But they didn't stop.

Throughout the party, the girls said and did things that Isabella knew were wrong. Isabella knew she was breaking her family's first rule: *Honor God in everything you say and do.*

She was relieved when her mom finally came back. Isabella felt sad and tired trying to make her friends happy. She wasn't sure it was worth it.

DECISION 2:

Isabella didn't like hearing the bad words, but she also didn't like the idea of losing her friends. So the next time one of the girls used a bad word, Isabella repeated it.

She had never said a word like that before, and it tasted bitter coming out of her mouth.

"Isabella!" said one of the girls. "I'm surprised! I didn't think you said words like that."

Isabella's eyes filled with tears. She had thought the group expected her to say the bad words, but instead they were shocked. And it didn't seem to earn her any extra approval.

She wished with all her heart she could take the word back.

DECISION 3:

Isabella didn't want to speak up and ask her friends to stop using the word, but she remembered her family's rules: *Honor God in everything you say and do. Tell the truth. Think of others. Say "thank you."*

Saying bad words was definitely *not* honoring God.

She took a deep breath. "Let's not say that word anymore, okay? I'm sure we can think of better words."

And to her surprise, her friends agreed. She was thankful.

WHY DOES IT MATTER?

The Bible tells us that the tongue is a small part of our body, yet it holds great power.

Our words can pierce and wound other people just like a sword. But they can also give life and bring health to others when they're suffering or sad.

When we say a bad word, it may not feel like a big deal. It's just a word—it's not meant to harm anything or anyone, right? But the Bible says that every word we say either honors or dishonors God.

Psalm 141:3 should be our prayer—"O Lord, put a watch over my mouth. Keep watch over the door of my lips."

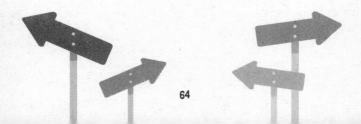

THE BEST SHORTCUT

Elijah loved doing whatever was easy, so he took short-cuts whenever possible.

When his mom told him to clean his room, he would just shove everything into his closet. When his dad sent him to run around the block for exercise, he would cut through the neighbor's backyard to shorten the distance. When it was his turn to wash the dishes, he would just wipe them with a dry dishcloth to avoid loading and unloading the dishwasher.

He was always happy to discover a new way to cut corners.

One day in math class, Elijah's teacher split the classroom into groups of two. Each pair of students was supposed to do the assignment and turn in their answers together.

Elijah was happy because even though he had no idea how to do it, he was paired with Willow, the smartest kid in class. All Elijah needed to do was sit back and let her do everything.

"A new shortcut!" he said with a grin as he walked toward Willow's desk.

But Willow knew Elijah well enough to know what he had planned. She turned to him and explained that letting her do all the work might earn a good grade now, but it wouldn't prepare him for the test. It would also put him behind in class, since math concepts build on each other.

Willow said that shortcuts don't always save time; sometimes they actually make life harder.

Elijah thought about it.

If you were Elijah, what would you do?

Decision 1: Let Willow do the assignment. Getting a good grade is the goal. (turn to page 67)

Decision 2: Pretend to work so Willow doesn't get mad, but let her find the answers. (turn to page 68)

Decision 3: Do the hard work along with Willow and learn how to do the assignment. (turn to page 69)

DECISION 1:

Elijah listened to what Willow said. He nodded and smiled. . .and then let her do the assignment anyway. His biggest goal in life was finding shortcuts, and he wasn't going to change that now. He knew Willow would get a good grade for both of them.

Sure enough, Elijah didn't learn how to do the math problems, and when the test came, he didn't know what to do. He failed the test and was clueless on the next chapter too. Now he would need to go back and start again.

DECISION 2:

When Willow was finished explaining why he needed to participate, Elijah began doodling. He didn't do any of the problems or ask any good questions, but he made Willow think he was working on the assignment. Willow wasn't upset because she thought he cared about his work.

When the math test arrived, Elijah failed it. Even though he got a good grade on the assignment, the test was worth much more. Elijah wished he had followed Willow's advice.

DECISION 3:

Elijah knew Willow was right. So instead of letting her do all the work, he pulled his chair next to hers and learned how to do the assignment. He didn't love doing the work, but he loved the satisfaction he got when they turned in the assignment and earned the good grade *together*. Even better: receiving a good grade on the test.

Elijah knew he should start rethinking his love of shortcuts. Maybe it was time to start actually cleaning his room, running for exercise, and cleaning the dishes. Maybe the best shortcut was doing work the right way.

WHY DOES IT MATTER?

The Bible teaches us that God loves hard work. In fact, work was part of God's original, good design. God gave Adam the important job of caring for the garden and the animals before sin ever entered the world.

A shortcut is anything we do to get a job done faster. Shortcuts aren't always bad, but when they keep us from doing our best work, they don't please God. Colossians 3:23 says, "Whatever work you do, do it with all your heart. Do it for the Lord and not for men."

Eleven

A CRASH COURSE IN KINDNESS

Harper had just one more lap to finish the race. The race had been long, and she was glad it was almost over. She and her fiercest competitor—Aubrey—were side by side, far ahead of the rest of the pack.

Harper had worked hard for this moment. Even though she wanted to quit, she pushed herself and pulled slightly ahead, but Aubrey did the same. It was going to be close. Harper and Aubrey were the best runners in the pack, and they were pushing each other to do better.

Harper could hear the cheers from her friends and family in the stands. She was barely ahead when suddenly—out of the corner of her eye—she saw a flash of movement. Aubrey had fallen!

With only a split second to act, Harper looked to see Aubrey lying on the ground, holding her leg and calling out for help. Something terrible had happened, and now she was in a lot of pain.

Harper considered running as fast as she could. She could easily win the race now.

But what about Aubrey? How could she leave her

lying on the ground?

What would be the point of winning the race if Aubrey was hurt? Should she stop and see how she could help, or should she take advantage of her chance to win?

She had only a moment to decide.

If you were Harper, what would you do?

Decision 1: Keep running, and let the adults help Aubrey. (turn to page 73)

Decision 2: Stop and see if Aubrey is okay. The race can wait. (turn to page 74)

Decision 3: Win the race and then come back to check on Aubrey. (turn to page 75)

DECISION 1:

Harper knew Aubrey was in pain and needed help, but she kept running. It wasn't her fault Aubrey had fallen. And besides, what could she do? Aubrey's coach and parents would help Aubrey off the track. This was finally Harper's chance to win!

A few moments later, Harper ran across the finish line and stopped to catch her breath. She had won! But the win didn't feel nearly as good as she thought it would. The crowd was focused on Aubrey, and the win felt empty.

DECISION 2:

Harper locked eyes with Aubrey and knew in that moment that winning didn't matter nearly as much as helping her competitor. She turned and ran to Aubrey, kneeling down beside her. "What can I do?" Harper asked.

"My leg!" Aubrey cried. Harper held Aubrey's hand until the coach arrived. She helped Aubrey's coach lift her off the track and take her to someone who could care for her leg.

When Harper finally turned back to the race, she saw that all the other competitors had stopped racing too. She realized in that moment that winning a race doesn't matter nearly as much as caring about someone in need.

DECISION 3:

Harper wanted to help Aubrey, but she also wanted to win. So she quickly formed a plan. She would finish the race and, after she had won, would go back to check on Aubrey.

She forced herself to pick up her speed and dashed across the finish line.

Hardly anyone clapped from the sidelines, making the win feel shallow.

When Harper turned back to help, she saw that Aubrey had already been moved off the track. Surrounding her were several other competitors, holding her hand and encouraging her.

Harper ran to where Aubrey and their competitors were huddled, but they didn't need her.

WHY DOES IT MATTER?

The Bible never tells us to stop a race when our competitor is injured, but it does tell us that we should always be deeply concerned with helping people in need.

In Luke 10 Jesus tells the story of the Good Samaritan. In this parable, a traveler is beaten and left to die on the side of the road. Two men travel by, but neither stop to help the man. Then a Samaritan passes by. Samaritans and Jews were known for hating each other—they were rivals in *every* sense. But the Samaritan man stops to help the injured man anyway. At the end of the story, Jesus says, "Go and do the same" (Luke 10:37).

Twelve

A FRIEND REQUEST

Chante's dad had a new job, which meant he and his family had to move from a big city to a small town. Chante had spent all his life in the city, where he had many friends and lots to do.

Now—in the small town—he had no friends and nothing to do.

His mom encouraged him to be kind to his classmates and to make friends at church. He tried, but so far nobody was interested in coming over or inviting him to their house to play. Everybody seemed to have friends already, and Chante wondered if he would ever feel at home there.

Chante was lonely. He wished his family could just pack up and move back to the city, where his friends would be waiting for him.

Then one Sunday, Chante heard the pastor read Deuteronomy 31:6, which says, "Be strong and have strength of heart. Do not be afraid or shake with fear because of them. For the Lord your God is the One Who goes with you. He will be faithful to you. He will not leave you alone."

He knew God promised to be his friend, but God felt so far away.

If you were Chante, what would you do?

Decision 1: Pray and ask God for friends in the new town while trusting that He will be a close friend in the meantime. (turn to page 79)

Decision 2: Ignore the loneliness. Who needs people anyway? (turn to page 80)

Decision 3: Be a friend to anyone who is willing—even if the person isn't the right kind of friend. (turn to page 81)

DECISION 1:

Chante was sitting in his room feeling lonely when he realized he could do something more productive. Instead of feeling sorry for himself, he decided to stop and pray about it. He knew that God cared about his desire for friends, so he started asking God to bring the right kind of friends into his life.

Not only did Chante get to experience the closeness of God, but it wasn't long until he started finding kids who needed his friendship as much as he needed theirs.

DECISION 2:

Chante decided he would stop looking for friends. It would be easier that way. Being alone was better than being rejected, right?

He started playing by himself and doing only the things *he* enjoyed. When kids tried talking to him, he ignored them and looked for ways to avoid everyone. All he cared about was himself.

The problem was that this new way of life didn't make him feel any better. He felt totally, completely *alone*. Even worse, he felt further away from God.

DECISION 3:

Chante wanted friends so badly that it hurt just to think about it. It seemed unfair to him that he had to leave his friends behind just so his dad could keep his job. Why wouldn't the kids here give him a chance?

Chante finally decided to take matters into his own hands. He was willing to make friends with anyone. He would even join the kids in the neighborhood who were always getting in trouble, as long as they would accept him.

The only problem? Chante learned soon enough that getting in trouble didn't feel any better than being lonely.

WHY DOES IT MATTER?

One of the greatest gifts God gives His children is the promise that we are never alone. Even when we feel lonely, He is with us.

Jesus is the friend who "stays nearer than a brother" (Proverbs 18:24).

El Shaddai is one of the many names of God in the Bible. In Hebrew it means "the God who is all-sufficient." This means whatever need we have—including the need for a friend—can be met by God. We get ourselves in trouble whenever we try to meet our own needs without God's help.

THIRTEEN

NEVER HURTS TO ASK

Mila knew she was supposed to pray to God every day. She had even memorized Philippians 4:6, which says, "Do not worry. Learn to pray about everything. Give thanks to God as you ask Him for what you need."

Her Sunday school teacher liked to quote 1 Thessalonians 5:17, "Never stop praying." He explained that this meant talking to God throughout the day whenever Mila needed God's help or wanted to thank Him for something.

But Mila had a problem.

She didn't think God answered her prayers very often.

For example, she had prayed that God would help her mom to either get a new job or have enough money to pay the bills. But the money wasn't coming in, and the bills were piling up. She had prayed for God to help her pass a test at school, but she had failed.

Mila didn't understand how prayer works or why she should do it. Praying only raised her hopes and then disappointed her.

Mila loved God very much, of course. But it was

easier for her *not* to pray than to ask God and learn that the answer was "No."

She decided she would figure prayer out when she was older.

Then Mila found out her dad was very sick. He would need to have surgery right away to save his life. Mila knew she should pray about it, but she was scared. What if God said "No" again? If He did, she was afraid she would never be able to trust Him.

If you were Mila, what would you do?

Decision 1: Pray and ask God for help. Trust Him to do what is best. (turn to page 85)

Decision 2: Refuse to pray about it—that way the answer can't be "No." (turn to page 86)

Decision 3: Keep praying, but only for the food at meal-times. (turn to page 87)

DECISION 1:

Mila decided her dad meant too much to her for her to stop praying now.

Her Sunday school teacher had shared Hebrews 4:16: "Let us go with complete trust to the throne of God. We will receive His loving-kindness and have His loving-favor to help us whenever we need it."

Even though she was scared, Mila prayed and asked God to help her trust Him. She also asked Him to help her parents. She knew asking God for help was *always* the right decision, no matter what happened in the future.

DECISION 2:

Mila decided to stop praying for a while.

Even though she knew the Bible told her to pray, she also knew how hard it would be if God said "No" to her again. She wondered if she would ever be able to trust Him if He refused to help her father.

But not praying made her sad too. She realized that talking to God in prayer was as much of a gift as receiving what she requested. By refusing to pray, she was only hurting herself.

DECISION 3:

Mila decided she couldn't entirely quit praying. People knew she was a Christian, and they would be confused if she stopped. So she prayed at meals. She said the usual things like "Thank You for this food" and "Help us to have a good day."

She was careful not to ask for anything that would hurt if God said, "No." She wanted to know without a doubt that God would say "Yes" to whatever she requested before she asked for anything important again.

Strangely, it didn't feel to Mila like she was truly praying. It felt more like she was just doing her duty or checking a box. She missed the times when she had truly talked to God.

WHY DOES IT MATTER?

God always wants us to pray. He wants us to live each day looking for reasons to talk to Him. James 5:13 says, "Is anyone among you suffering? He should pray. Is anyone happy? He should sing songs of thanks to God." God wants us to talk constantly to Him.

The only thing worse than receiving a "No" from God is receiving no answer at all because we've refused to talk to Him. God loves us and will always give us the best answer. So next time you have a prayer request or feel thankful, stop what you're doing and talk to God!

Fourteen

NEVER TAKE "SIN" FOR AN ANSWER

Ethan wanted with all his heart to go to summer camp with his church friends. He had heard how wonderful it was to learn about God while meeting new people. At night all he could think about was getting to camp and making great memories.

He knew going to camp wasn't cheap, so he did everything he could—washing cars, pulling weeds, and mowing lawns—to earn money. As he worked, he asked God to provide the money for him to go. He knew God could make a way, since He owned all the money in the world.

One morning, he discovered John 14:13 while reading the Bible. It says, "Whatever you ask in My name, I will do it so the shining-greatness of the Father may be seen in the Son." This verse excited him because he trusted God to provide.

Later, while he was mowing Mrs. Johnson's yard, he spotted a lump of leather in the grass. He stopped the mower and went to get a closer look.

It was a wallet, and it was packed with money!

Counting the bills, he knew right away it was more

than enough money for him to go to camp. He looked around but didn't see anyone looking for a wallet. And there was nothing inside that revealed its owner.

Was this the answer to his prayer? Maybe God had allowed him to find the wallet so he'd have enough money to go to camp!

If you were Ethan, what would you do?

Decision 1: Keep the money and thank God for providing a way to go to camp. (turn to page 91)

Decision 2: Find the owner and return the wallet. (turn to page 92)

Decision 3: Put the money in the offering plate at church. It belongs to God anyway. (turn to page 93)

DECISION 1:

Ethan decided to keep the wallet, even though a voice inside him said he should find the owner. He ignored the voice, reminding himself that he had been praying for God to provide what he needed. *What if this wallet is God's answer?*

Now that he had enough money to go to camp, he quit doing extra jobs or daydreaming about camp. Instead of praying and working, he started imagining all the fun ways he could spend his money.

Soon, he completely quit caring about camp and decided to buy a new gaming system.

DECISION 2:

Ethan wanted to keep the wallet. He knew the money would be more than enough, but he also felt wrong about keeping what didn't belong to him. Even though it was tempting, Ethan knew stealing couldn't be the answer to his prayer.

He knew there must be a better way.

Ethan knocked on Mrs. Johnson's door and told her what had happened. She was relieved to hear he had found the wallet, because her grandson had lost it the night before. Since Ethan had been honest, Mrs. Johnson offered to pay his way to camp. Ethan was awestruck at the way God provided.

DECISION 3:

At first, Ethan decided to keep the money, but as time passed, he didn't feel right about it. In fact, it made him sick whenever he remembered the wallet in his pocket. He began to think maybe keeping the money *wasn't* the answer to his prayer.

On Sunday, he was tired of thinking about it, so he dropped the wallet—with all the money inside—into the offering plate at church.

It was God's money anyway, right?

He had hoped getting rid of the wallet would make him feel better, but it only made him feel worse when his parents asked him about it later. He should have talked to them at the beginning!

WHY DOES IT MATTER?

Sometimes when we want something from God, it's easy to take matters into our own hands.

In Numbers 20, Moses made the terrible mistake of trying to answer his prayer by doing things his own way. The people of Israel needed water, so God told Moses to speak to a rock, which would produce water and show God's power and glory.

Instead of speaking, Moses hit the rock with a stick—twice! Water flowed, but Moses lost his chance to enter the Promised Land.

It's never right to do the wrong thing, even if it means getting the chance to do right.

FiFTeeN

THANKS OR NO THANKS

It was Christmas morning, and Ella was very excited. In fact, she was so excited she had hardly slept that night. Today she would finally get to open her Christmas gift!

She had asked for only one toy this year—a wooden dollhouse. After discovering it in a toy catalog and circling it with every marker she owned, she had talked about it nonstop for weeks.

Ella had already imagined all the ways she would decorate it, and had even cleared a spot for it in her bedroom. She knew her friends would love playing with it as much as she did.

Today was finally the day!

She raced downstairs to where the gifts waited under the Christmas tree. Ella and her brother searched until they found their own boxes. Her box was the biggest! She tore the wrapping away. . .*and it wasn't a dollhouse.*

It was just a cloth doll with yarn hair.

She stared at it for a moment, trying to decide what to say. Ella knew her parents were excited to give it to her. She felt them watching her, and she knew they would ask her to pose for a picture whenever she looked up. This had been a hard year on the family, and they had bought her the best gift they could afford.

But Ella was still disappointed. Why couldn't she have received the one gift she had requested?

If you were Ella, what would you do?

Decision 1: Be honest about the gift being a disappointment. Refuse to play with the doll. (turn to page 97)

Decision 2: Tell your parents this is exactly what you wanted to avoid hurting their feelings. (turn to page 98)

Decision 3: Thank your parents for loving you enough to give you a gift on Christmas. (turn to page 99)

DECISION 1:

Ella dropped the doll back into the box as her eyes filled with hot tears. She was a hardworking, obedient daughter who had asked for only one thing this Christmas while her friends had long lists of gifts. She *deserved* to get the wooden dollhouse.

"Do you like it, honey?" her dad asked.

In response, she pushed herself up and stomped to her room even as her parents called after her. Ella knew this reaction would hurt their feelings, but she didn't care.

Without the dollhouse, Christmas was ruined.

DECISION 2:

Ella stared at the doll for a long moment. It was not what she wanted, but she didn't want to hurt anybody's feelings. She pasted a fake smile on her face and looked at her parents. "Thank you!" she said as cheerfully as she could. "This is exactly what I wanted!"

"Really?" her mom asked. "We thought you wanted a dollhouse."

Ella shrugged. "This is great!"

But even as she said the words, she felt angry. It was hard being both disappointed *and* fake. But what other choice did she have?

DECISION 3:

Ella stared at the doll, silently praying for the courage to respond correctly. She knew her parents didn't have a lot of money and that they would have gotten the dollhouse for her if they could.

"Let's see it!" her mom said, holding the camera up for yet another photo.

Ella held up the doll for a photo. "Thank you for giving me a Christmas gift," she said. "I love you."

She wouldn't lie and say it was exactly what she wanted, but she also wouldn't ruin their relationship over a toy. Relationships matter more than dollhouses.

WHY DOES IT MATTER?

Life can be disappointing, but God makes a big promise to His children in Psalm 34:10—"The young lions suffer want and hunger. But they who look for the Lord will not be without any good thing."

When we suffer disappointments in this life, we can be sure God knows and cares.

We can also know He has a good plan for our lives. So whenever we don't get something we want we can trust that it's part of His perfect plan.

Sixteen

YOU ARE INVITED!

It was Friday night, and Henry was the only one at home with his parents. Each of Henry's three brothers was out having fun with friends.

His oldest brother was at a basketball game.

His younger brother had gone to a sleepover.

His youngest brother was at a birthday party at a bowling alley.

All these things sounded fun to Henry, but he was stuck at home with nothing to do.

He didn't want to play games. He didn't want to watch movies. He didn't want to read. All he wanted to do was spend time with friends, just like his brothers were doing.

When Henry told his dad how unfair everything felt, his dad said, "Sometimes life is unfair."

His dad loved to say that.

Henry's dad often talked about kids in other countries who didn't have family, friends, or food. But Henry didn't want to hear it tonight.

Life should be fair for everyone, shouldn't it?

Why were some kids not invited to birthday parties?

Why did some kids fail to make the sports teams? Why did some kids get to buy new toys and clothes, while other kids got nothing? Why were some kids good at everything, while other kids seemed to struggle?

It's just not fair!

"Son," his dad finally said, "you need to have a good attitude, even when life feels unfair. We can't choose our circumstances, but we can always choose our attitude."

If you were Henry, what would you do?

Decision 1: Sulk for the rest of the evening. Sometimes it just feels good to be cranky. (turn to page 103)
Decision 2: Quit caring about everything. It's harder to get hurt when you've quit caring. (turn to page 104)
Decision 3: Look for ways to make Friday evening better. (turn to page 105)

DECISION 1:

Henry was mad, bored, and cranky, and he didn't want to change how he felt. He believed he should have been invited to do something fun with his friends, but since he was stuck at home, he decided he would just sulk for the rest of the night.

When his parents tried to cheer him up, he got angrier.

If Henry thought he was hurting everyone else with his attitude, he was wrong. He thought he'd feel better if he sulked, but he just felt worse.

He had ruined his own Friday night, and even worse, he had failed to please God.

DECISION 2:

Henry knew he'd get into trouble with his parents if he kept sulking, but he didn't want to cheer up either. He still thought it was unfair that he wasn't doing something fun on a Friday night.

So he decided to quit caring about everything. If he didn't care, he couldn't get hurt, right? He hoped not caring would be like a superpower.

Who cares about friends?

Who cares about invitations?

Who cares about being liked or accepted?

Except he did care, and pretending he didn't only made him feel worse.

DECISION 3:

Henry knew the only way to stop feeling bad about his boring Friday night was by looking for a way to make it better. So he sat on his bed and thought about what he could do.

Suddenly he remembered Mr. Keith.

Mr. Keith was Henry's elderly neighbor who never got to go anywhere or do anything fun. Henry thought about how lonely that must be, so he decided to visit Mr. Keith. He had such a fun evening hearing Mr. Keith's stories that he forgot about his own worries.

WHY DOES IT MATTER?

Life doesn't always feel good. Being left out hurts, and sometimes we can feel lonely or forgotten. The easiest way to fix this problem isn't to just be happy or quit caring—the Bible doesn't support either of these choices.

Instead, God calls us to tell Him about our disappointments and to care about others.

Luke 6:31 says, "Do for other people what you would like to have them do for you."

If you're feeling sad or disappointed today, whom can you encourage? Maybe that person is waiting for *you* to care.

SEVENTEEN

ON THE HUNT

It was time for the yearly Easter egg hunt, and Lyla was excited because she was the fastest and strongest kid in attendance, and she knew she could easily collect more eggs if she hurried.

Lyla stood on the line, clutching her basket and looking out at the field where hundreds of eggs were waiting. Each egg contained a piece of candy or a tiny toy, and her goal was to get at least one hundred, even if it meant other kids didn't get as many. If they didn't hurry, it would be their loss!

Lyla looked around to see her competition.

To her left was a girl from class named Camila. Camila had braces on her legs that made walking—and especially running—much harder. To Lyla's right were the younger kids, standing nervously beside their parents.

I'm the fastest one here! she thought.

The man in charge of the hunt announced that it was almost time to start. He reminded the kids that they should have fun but also seek to be like Jesus.

What does that mean? This is a competition. The goal

should be to get as many eggs as possible, no matter what!

The man counted backward from ten and blew his whistle.

Children spilled onto the field with baskets in hand.

If you were Lyla, what would you do?

Decision 1: Get as many eggs as possible! It's a competition. (turn to page 109)

Decision 2: Give everyone a few seconds' head start and then dive in and take everything else. (turn to page 110)

Decision 3: Take a fair amount and then offer to help others. (turn to page 111)

DECISION 1:

Lyla ran, elbowing past everyone and grabbing as many eggs as she could. She grabbed eggs right out from under people and laughed as she ran away, filling her basket and her pockets and the hood of her sweatshirt.

At the end of the hunt, she was sure she had more than a hundred eggs. She knew there were kids who didn't get many, but it wasn't her fault she was so fast!

When the man in charge blew his whistle to signal that the hunt had ended, Lyla was sad. She wanted even *more* eggs. Even though she had the most, it wasn't enough!

DECISION 2:

Lyla held back for a moment and let everyone else run first. She knew she'd easily be able to collect all the eggs she wanted, but she'd feel better about it if she let everyone else get a head start.

After a few seconds, she tore onto the field, ready to win.

She knocked kids over, collected as many eggs as possible, and gloated when the hunt was over.

Strangely, nobody wanted to talk to her afterward—not even her friends.

She started to think maybe collecting so many eggs wasn't worth it.

DECISION 3:

Lyla ran and filled her basket with eggs. She considered taking more, but then she saw kids who didn't have many yet. She might be allowed to take all the eggs she wanted, but she knew Jesus wouldn't do that if He were in her place. So when Lyla noticed a little girl collecting eggs all by herself, she did what she thought Jesus would do. She offered to help.

To Lyla's surprise, it was even more fun collecting eggs for someone else!

WHY DOES IT MATTER?

Doing what's allowed and doing what's best are different things.

Jesus set the ultimate example for us by always honoring His Father and thinking of others. Jesus didn't seek to *get* the most, but to *give* the most. In fact, He even gave His life for us.

The Bible says, "Think as Christ Jesus thought. Jesus has always been as God is. But He did not hold to His rights as God. He put aside everything that belonged to Him and made Himself the same as a servant who is owned by someone" (Philippians 2:5–7).

Let's hunt for opportunities to be like Jesus.

Eighteen

WHAT A KID NEEDS

Owen arrived at camp with twenty-five dollars in his pocket. He was *so* excited. He never had much money, but now he had twenty-five dollars all to himself.

He knew he could easily spend it in a single day. Just imagine all the candy and snacks he could buy! And nobody was around to tell him, "No," or, "Save your money for later." Owen could buy whatever he wanted whenever he wanted it.

So he went to the snack shop.

As Owen stared at all the rows of candy and treats, he wondered what to buy first. At home, he wasn't allowed to have many sugary drinks, so he started filling his basket with some of those first. And then he came to the candy bars and chips.

That was when he heard two people talking in the next aisle.

They were discussing the collection that would be taken later that week for kids in need around the world.

What do these kids need? he wondered. So he listened a little closer.

He learned that many children around the world

didn't have families to take care of them, and many went without food. Even worse, many children didn't know anything about Jesus or how much He loves them.

A missionary couple was visiting camp and taking up a collection of money later that week to help as many kids as possible learn about Jesus.

Owen had a feeling in the pit of his stomach that he shouldn't just waste all his money on himself. But then he remembered how excited he was about spending the twenty-five dollars. He glanced down at his basket of goodies.

If you were Owen, what would you do?

Decision 1: Put everything back. Buying anything would be selfish. (turn to page 115)
Decision 2: Put some of it back and give some of the money to kids in need. (turn to page 116)
Decision 3: Buy all the candy and goodies. Camp happens only once a year. Ask Mom and Dad to give a donation. (turn to page 117)

DECISION 1:

Owen couldn't shake the idea that some children had nothing while he had so much. So he emptied his basket—putting everything back on the shelves where it belonged—and went back to his cabin. He decided he would never again enjoy anything he didn't need. He wouldn't accept gifts or eat treats or have fun.

If other kids couldn't enjoy good things, he wouldn't enjoy them either.

His camp counselor tried to explain that it was possible to enjoy what we have while sharing with others, but Owen wouldn't listen. He just wanted to go home and forget about camp.

DECISION 2:

Owen knew he should do something to help kids in need. Standing in the aisle, he closed his eyes and silently prayed for God to show him what to do. When he finished, he realized he should give some of what he had, so Owen returned half the items in his basket. He would take part of the money and put it in the collection.

More importantly, he would talk to his parents about what else he could do to continue caring about kids who needed to hear the Gospel.

DECISION 3:

Owen felt sorry for the needy kids, but they weren't his responsibility. He had twenty-five dollars to spend, and he was going to spend it on himself. When he got home he would ask his parents to make a donation. After all, they had a lot more money.

He took his basket of goodies up to the counter and paid.

When he got back to his cabin, he dumped everything out on his bed.

But suddenly, it didn't seem as exciting now. He couldn't stop thinking about what he could have done with some of his money.

WHY DOES IT MATTER?

James 1:17 tells us that God is a loving Father, giving us good and perfect gifts and wanting us to enjoy them. But He also wants us to live unselfishly and help people who are in need.

We must remember that everything we have belongs to God. Even when we think we are giving *our* money to God, the truth is that it all belongs to *Him*.

Instead of being controlled by what we have, we should use what we've been given to glorify God.

Nineteen

NOT TO WORRY

Jillian lay in her bed late at night, listening to her sister snore beside her. She knew she should be asleep too, but she couldn't stop thinking about something.

Years earlier, when Jillian was only four years old, she had trusted Jesus as her Savior at vacation Bible school. But now she struggled with doubt. She wondered if she had made the right decision, or if she had even understood enough to be saved.

Every night, she struggled with fear.

Fear loomed in her room like a big, scary monster, just waiting for her to go to bed. She would think terrible thoughts about an eternity without Christ. Her heart would race, her stomach would hurt, and her eyes would fill with tears.

Jillian knew her parents could help her, but she wondered if they would be upset or disappointed. She had already been baptized, and everyone assumed she followed Jesus. What if she disappointed everyone?

Sometimes she would get up in the morning exhausted from a long night of worrying about what would happen if she wasn't really a Christian. But then she would try her best to forget about it. . .until night came again.

One morning, Jillian's mom saw her sitting at the kitchen table with her head down. She said, "Jillian, you've looked sad a lot lately. What's wrong? Can we talk about it?"

Jillian knew this was her chance to tell her mom what was happening and ask for help, but she also knew it would require courage.

If you were Jillian, what would you do?

Decision 1: Refuse to say anything so nobody gets upset. Deal with it alone. (turn to page 121)
Decision 2: Talk to Mom and trust she will be helpful and understanding. (turn to page 122)
Decision 3: Ignore the feeling of fear and hope it goes away. (turn to page 123)

DECISION 1:

Jillian stared at her mom and considered telling her the truth. It would feel good to get the truth out in the open, but her mom looked like she might already be having a bad morning. Jillian didn't want to upset her further.

"I'm fine," Jillian said, digging her spoon into her cereal. "I just didn't sleep well last night."

"Okay," her mom said, turning back to what she was doing.

Jillian could tell it would be yet another long night, and she already dreaded going to bed. If only she had told her mom the truth. . . .

DECISION 2:

Jillian considered telling her mom she was fine, but she knew this chance might never come again. She needed to trust her mom to help her.

She began to cry. "Mom, I don't know if I was ready to trust Christ when I was four. I'm worried I'm not truly saved."

Her mom looked confused for a moment, but then she sat down at the table next to Jillian. With tears in her own eyes, her mom said, "Then let's talk and pray about it together."

These were exactly the words Jillian needed to hear. She was thankful she had been honest.

DECISION 3:

Jillian cared about nothing more than making her parents happy. She did everything—from cleaning her room to making good grades—to please them. So Jillian decided not to say anything about her fear.

"Nothing's wrong," Jillian said brightly. "Can I help you clear the table?"

Her mom looked at her for a moment, but then she eventually nodded.

Jillian decided the best way to handle her fear was to pretend it didn't exist.

The problem? She could tell already that it wouldn't go away.

WHY DOES IT MATTER?

Many of us have had doubts or fears about whether we are truly saved. This is absolutely normal. But the Bible tells us that "God did not give us a spirit of fear. He gave us a spirit of power and of love and of a good mind" (2 Timothy 1:7).

Whenever you feel frightened or confused, ask God to give you the courage to talk about it to your parents, grandparents, or teachers from church. You may be surprised at how willing they are to help.

TWENTY

SEVENTY TIMES SEVEN

One Sunday, Grayson's best friend, Joey, did something really hurtful. He laughed at Grayson in front of the entire Sunday school class for giving a wrong answer during Bible trivia.

The question: What type of insect did John the Baptist eat in the desert?

The answer: Locusts.

But instead of *locusts*, Grayson said, "Frogs."

Joey thought it was an easy question, so he laughed at Grayson for "being so dumb."

Because of Grayson's wrong answer, his team lost the trivia competition, and Joey told everyone it was Grayson's fault.

Grayson was embarrassed and sad that his wrong answer had hurt his team, but he was also hurt that Joey would be so mean.

He decided a true friend wouldn't do something so unkind. Maybe Joey wasn't a true friend after all.

After church, Joey asked Grayson if they could talk. Joey explained that he knew what he had done was unkind, and he apologized. He explained that God had convicted him during the sermon, and he knew he needed to make things right. He asked Grayson to forgive him and give him another chance. Joey promised not to do it again.

The problem? Grayson wasn't sure he wanted to forgive him. They had been close friends for many years, so Joey should have known better. Grayson thought Joey should have to pay for what he did. Forgiving him would only let Joey off the hook.

Grayson told Joey he would need to think about it for a while.

If you were Grayson, what would you do?

Decision 1: Forgive him and give him another chance. (turn to page 127)
Decision 2: Refuse to forgive Joey. He needs to learn an important lesson. (turn to page 128)
Decision 3: Forgive Joey but make him pay for it. Forgiveness isn't cheap. (turn to page 129)

DECISION 1:

Grayson was hurt, but he also knew that he too was a sinner who sometimes made mistakes. Grayson thought about the many ways he had hurt other people—like his parents and his sister—and he knew it would be wrong to want forgiveness from them while refusing to forgive Joey.

Grayson believed God wanted him to forgive. In Sunday school he had learned Ephesians 4:32, "You must be kind to each other. Think of the other person. Forgive other people just as God forgave you because of Christ's death on the cross."

He told Joey he would give him another chance.

DECISION 2:

Grayson was hurt by what Joey had done, so he decided he would never forgive Joey. Their friendship was over. He thought this would teach Joey an important lesson about how to treat his friends.

Grayson told Joey his decision, but he didn't feel better about it.

The next Sunday at church he saw Joey sitting and talking with other kids, and Grayson realized he missed his friend. He also thought about the ways he had hurt his own friends and family.

Maybe he should have forgiven Joey. Was it too late?

DECISION 3:

Grayson told Joey he would forgive him.

But then he made Joey pay for what he had done. He laughed whenever Joey made mistakes, and he reminded Joey as often as possible that he had been hurtful. He didn't invite Joey to his birthday party, and he made sure Joey knew that he had other friends he liked better.

Soon, Grayson realized he and Joey weren't really friends anymore.

Grayson wondered if these choices were actually worse than what Joey had done during the trivia game.

WHY DOES IT MATTER?

As humans, we sometimes hurt people and get hurt by others. God isn't pleased when this happens, but He doesn't want us to grow bitter or angry either. He wants us to forgive.

In the New Testament, the apostle Peter asked Jesus how often he should forgive the people who hurt him. Jesus replied, "I tell you, not seven times but seventy times seven!" (Matthew 18:22).

It's important that we make wise and safe decisions, so sometimes forgiveness also means we must be careful around someone who hurt us before. Thankfully, we can trust God and our parents to help us make wise choices.

We should forgive others like God forgives us.

Twenty-One

WAIT FOR IT

Stella hated waiting.

She hated waiting for summer vacation.

She hated waiting for Christmas and birthdays to arrive.

She hated waiting for cookies to bake, and she especially hated how long it took to grow up. Every day of her childhood felt like an eternity.

Stella couldn't wait until she was a grown-up. She'd be able to go anywhere, eat anything, and do everything she wanted. She could spend her money however she wished with no adults to tell her what to do. She wouldn't have to go to bed early, and she would never need to worry about homework again.

Wouldn't that be a wonderful life?

Stella thought adulthood sounded like a dream come true.

Her grandma always said that "everything good takes time," but Stella didn't want to wait. She was impatient in every way.

If only she could just snap her fingers and make good things happen! She would make herself older, give herself lots of money, and make sure she had everything she wanted right away.

Life would be so much better that way.

One day after Stella's birthday, as she was already dreaming of her *next* birthday, her mom advised her to slow down and enjoy her childhood.

"Lord willing, you'll have plenty of time to grow up," her mom said. "And being an adult isn't quite as easy as you think it is."

But Stella wasn't sure she wanted to enjoy being a kid when there was so much to look forward to. Childhood was just a bunch of waiting.

If you were Stella, what would you do?

Decision 1: Learn to be more patient about things like birthdays and holidays, but keep rushing through school to get it done. (turn to page 133)
Decision 2: Keep rushing to adulthood as fast as possible. (turn to page 134)
Decision 3: Slow down and appreciate each day. (turn to page 135)

DECISION 1:

Stella knew she should be more patient, but she also didn't want to slow down. So she compromised. She decided she would be more patient about birthdays and holidays (instead of always counting how many days were left until the next big event), but she would keep rushing through school. She just wanted to get it done.

It wasn't long before Stella realized that rushing through school only made it feel longer and less enjoyable. Being discontent about where God had placed her only made her more frustrated.

DECISION 2:

Stella knew her mom meant well, but she also thought her mom had probably forgotten how it felt to be a kid. So she decided to keep rushing through childhood as fast as she could. She counted down the days until her next birthday, and she made Christmas lists right after New Year's. Instead of doing her homework or studying for tests, she daydreamed about what life would be like when she was older.

Stella soon realized that she was never enjoying any events in her life because she was always looking forward to the next one.

DECISION 3:

Stella finally decided to slow down and appreciate the life God had given her. She wanted to be an adult, but she knew it would happen in God's perfect timing, and she didn't want to miss out on the good gifts God had for her in the meantime.

To help her appreciate each day, Stella began writing down one thing every morning for which she was grateful. Soon she had a whole notebook full of things like *time with Dad*, *a good grade in history*, *a new friend at school*, and so much more.

She would have missed these things if she hadn't slowed down!

WHY DOES IT MATTER?

Contentment isn't just something we feel—it's something we decide. Contentment means trusting that we have everything we need.

Being content isn't just something we learn as a kid. Contentment is necessary for every stage of life. The easiest way to learn contentment is found in Proverbs 3:5—"Trust in the Lord with all your heart, and do not trust in your own understanding."

We must trust that the story God is writing for us is a good one—and that we are always in the right chapter at the right time.

Twenty-Two

READY, SET, GO!

Lincoln loved to go to church. . .most of the time.

Sometimes he preferred to sleep in or go to a baseball game on Sunday mornings instead. And since his family didn't go to church, he knew the choice was ultimately up to him.

If he felt like skipping, he skipped.

If he felt like going, he went.

The more he studied the Bible, however, the more he believed God wanted him to go to church to worship Him instead of just doing whatever he wanted.

Lincoln decided he would start going to church every Sunday. He realized nothing—not even sleeping in or going to a baseball game—was better than singing praises to God and learning from God's Word.

While Lincoln was getting ready the next Sunday morning, his brother, Davis, came into his bedroom. "Lincoln," Davis said excitedly, "I've got tickets to the rodeo this morning. Want to go?"

Lincoln was shocked!

He had always wanted to go to a rodeo. In fact, he had been praying for a chance to see the rodeo if it ever came to town. For years, he and his brother had dreamed about watching the bull riding and steer wrestling, and now they finally had the chance!

If you were Lincoln, what would you do?

Decision 1: Go to church to show God that worshipping Him is even better than a rodeo. (turn to page 139)
Decision 2: Skip church just one more time to go to the rodeo. Is it really a big deal? (turn to page 140)
Decision 3: Go to Sunday school and then go to the rodeo during the church service. (turn to page 141)

DECISION 1:

Lincoln wanted to go to the rodeo, but he wanted to please God even more. So he made the tough decision to skip the rodeo and go to church instead. This decision gave Lincoln the chance to tell Davis again how much God meant to him. Davis didn't understand, but he respected Lincoln for taking his faith so seriously.

Lincoln decided to keep asking God for a chance to go to the rodeo. He trusted that there would be another opportunity, and even if there wasn't, he knew he was making the right decision.

DECISION 2:

Lincoln decided he would skip church just one more time to enjoy the rodeo. He and Davis headed out as soon as they could, and they spent the whole morning and afternoon together. They watched the events, ate the food, and enjoyed the music.

"Hey," Davis said to Lincoln. "Why do you go to church anyway? You obviously enjoy going to the rodeo even more."

Lincoln wanted to answer that God was most important in his life, but how could he say that when he was willing to skip church for a rodeo?

He wished he had gone to church first.

DECISION 3:

Lincoln told Davis he would go to Sunday school first and then leave for the rodeo. He invited Davis to go with him, but Davis just laughed and said that church wasn't his thing.

The entire time Lincoln was in Sunday school he kept watching the clock and thinking about how excited he was for the rodeo. His mind wasn't on the Bible at all.

As soon as class ended, he raced home.

"What'd you learn today?" Davis asked, but Lincoln couldn't respond. All he had thought of was the rodeo.

WHY DOES IT MATTER?

God wants us to regularly spend time with His people.

Hebrews 10:25 says, "Let us not stay away from church meetings. Some people are doing this all the time. Comfort each other as you see the day of His return coming near."

Sometimes we may need to miss a church service for work, sickness, or travel. But we should always remember that missing church comes with a cost. Sometimes the cost might be a missed opportunity to share our faith with family or friends. At other times we might miss out on learning an important lesson about God.

We show God how much He matters to us when we make worship a priority!

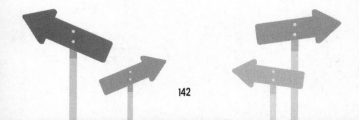

TWENTY-THREE

WINNER WINNER CHICKEN DINNER!

Kennedy stood up to the microphone at the spelling bee and waited for her word.

Butterflies fluttered in her stomach, and her heart raced.

She and Jose were the only students left, and Kennedy knew she could win the entire district spelling bee if she tried hard enough.

Jose misspelled his last word, so now it was all up to Kennedy.

So far, the words had been easy, and she was feeling hopeful.

But it all came down to this final word. . . .

"Onomatopoeia," the pronouncer called.

It was a big word, but Kennedy was ready. She took a deep breath and spelled it slowly.

"Correct!" the judge said.

The room erupted with cheers. Kennedy had won! She had dreamed of this moment for a long time, and now all her hard work had paid off. She saw a photographer from the local newspaper approaching her—as well as friends and family who had been in the audience watching—and she knew it was time to enjoy her victory.

She turned to see Jose sitting in his chair fighting back tears.

Nobody was talking to him. He was all alone.

Jose had worked just as hard as she had, so he could have easily been today's winner. She was about to go over and talk to him for a minute, but then she remembered—Jose hadn't always been kind to her. If he had won, he probably wouldn't have cared about cheering *her* up. Kennedy knew she needed to decide quickly.

If you were Kennedy, what would you do?

Decision 1: Go to Jose and tell him he did a good job and was a good competitor. (turn to page 145)

Decision 2: Enjoy being the winner and don't worry about Jose. He could have won, but he didn't. (turn to page 146)

Decision 3: Tell Jose that someday—if he worked harder—he could be a winner too. (turn to page 147)

DECISION 1:

Kennedy knew she should say something to encourage Jose because that's what Jesus would do. So she walked up to him, smiled kindly, and said, "You did a great job today. I really didn't think I'd be able to beat you. Thanks for the good competition."

To her surprise, Jose smiled. "Thanks," he said. "You deserved to win. Congratulations!"

When Kennedy learned that Jose's family hadn't come to watch him compete, she invited him to join her family in getting ice cream.

Not only did she win a competition, but she gained a friend.

DECISION 2:

Kennedy thought she should say something kind to Jose, but she *really* wanted to just enjoy winning. She had worked long and hard for this moment, and now her friends and family were ready to celebrate her.

She decided not to think about Jose anymore.

She hugged her parents, took pictures with her friends, and talked about how nervous she had been. When it was time to go, she told her parents to wait. She knew she should talk to Jose.

But when Kennedy turned around. . .he was gone.

She had missed an opportunity.

DECISION 3:

Kennedy was excited to celebrate her victory, but she knew she should say something to Jose first. People were watching her, and she wanted to look like she cared.

Walking up to Jose, she smiled and said as sweetly as she could, "Good job today. Maybe if you work harder next year, you could be a winner too."

She knew her words had sounded wrong when she saw the hurt in his eyes, but now it was time for her to enjoy being with her friends and family.

Kennedy had earned this victory, and that was all that mattered.

WHY DOES IT MATTER?

Just as it's important that we learn to lose properly, it's equally important that we learn to be good winners. This means being friendly, showing kindness, and giving grace.

Philippians 2:3 says, "Nothing should be done because of pride or thinking about yourself. Think of other people as more important than yourself."

Whether we win or lose a competition, we should care more about our opponent than about our performance. The true winner isn't the person who wins the competition, but rather the one who brings glory to God.

TWENTY-FOUR

KNOWING WHEN TO QUIT

With only three weeks left in the school year, Asher was shocked and excited to learn that he had straight As in his classes!

Normally, Asher was happy to get Bs and Cs in his classes, but he had worked hard this year, and now all that hard work was paying off. He knew his parents and grandparents would be so proud of him. They were always challenging him to work harder and do better.

As he looked at his grades, he realized something amazing—even if he didn't try his best for the rest of the year, he would still pass!

What an incredible feeling!

Looking at his homework that night, he really didn't want to do any of it. And why should he? He was tired of reading, studying, and writing all the time. He had spent the past several months doing schoolwork, and all he wanted to do now was play video games or visit the neighborhood kids. Spring had already arrived, so he wanted to quit caring about school.

I've earned it! he thought. *I deserve to forget about school and just have fun!*

He had done his best, but now he was finished.

Since he had good grades, he knew he could skip a few assignments and still be okay. Sure, his grades would go down—and he probably wouldn't end up with straight As—but he'd still pass. And that's what mattered most, right?

If you were Asher, what would you do?

Decision 1: Keep doing your best no matter what. (turn to page 151)

Decision 2: Skip the assignments and enjoy your time off. (turn to page 152)

Decision 3: At least do the homework—even if it isn't done well—so you have something to turn in. (turn to page 153)

DECISION 1:

Asher didn't want to do his homework, but he knew God wanted him to always do his best. So even though it was nice outside, Asher sat down and worked on his assignments.

His decision paid off a few weeks later when Asher saw that his report card was filled with As. He was thankful he hadn't given up at the last minute. Nothing felt as good as doing his best for the Lord.

DECISION 2:

Asher decided he wouldn't do his homework. Instead, he would let his hard work pay off, enjoying the last three weeks of school by not doing anything. He played games, hung out with his friends, and got a head start on summer break. He had fun!

But then he was shocked and disappointed when he received his report card. It was filled with Bs and Cs—just like his old ones had been.

He realized he shouldn't have given up so soon!

DECISION 3:

Asher knew it'd be wrong for him to completely skip his assignments, but he also didn't want to take the time to do them well. He decided if he at least had something to turn in, he'd be okay. So he rushed through his work every night and turned it in on time.

Many of his answers were fast, sloppy, and wrong.

Three weeks later, when he received his report card, he was disappointed to see that most of his As had fallen to Bs. At the bottom, his teacher had written a note: *You shouldn't have given up so soon!*

WHY DOES IT MATTER?

Whether you're doing schoolwork, cleaning your room, finishing chores, or helping someone in need, you have an important job to do.

One of the worst things you can do is quit.

Ecclesiastes 9:10 says, "Whatever your hand finds to do, do it with all your strength."

Even more important than making a good grade is honoring God. And God is not honored when we give up.

"Do not let yourselves get tired of doing good. If we do not give up, we will get what is coming to us at the right time" (Galatians 6:9).

Twenty-Five

GIVE TILL IT HELPS

One Sunday at church, Linnea heard the terrible news that her friend Aiysha had lost everything she owned in a house fire the night before. The church was collecting donations to help Aiysha and her family.

"Honey," Linnea's mom said on the ride home. "I'm planning to give some of my clothes and dishes to Aiysha's mom. I think it'd be great if you gave Aiysha some of your clothes and toys. Do you think you could pick out a few things?"

Linnea nodded.

She felt terrible that her friend was going through something so difficult. She couldn't imagine how sad and terrifying it must be.

Linnea would be happy to share with her.

Standing in her room that afternoon, Linnea wondered what she should give Aiysha. She looked through her belongings, trying to find the dresses and sweaters she liked the least. Maybe she could also part with a doll or two that she wasn't playing with anymore.

"I could give her the games that are missing pieces!" she said.

Linnea hated those games anyway. This was the perfect chance to get rid of them!

But then she thought about everything Aiysha's family was experiencing. Aiysha had lost all of her favorite toys and clothes. Would giving her a bunch of old clothes and broken toys really mean anything?

Linnea looked back at her closet and started rethinking what she should do.

Should she pick out the best things for Aiysha, or should she choose the items she had quit caring about?

If you were Linnea, what would you do?

Decision 1: Give Aiysha a few things that aren't favorites or don't fit anymore. She'll probably be happy with anything. (turn to page 157)

Decision 2: Give Aiysha a couple of old toys and a couple of new outfits. (turn to page 158)

Decision 3: Give Aiysha some of the best clothes and toys in the closet. (turn to page 159)

DECISION 1:

Linnea knew Aiysha would probably be happy with whatever she gave her.

It was better than nothing, right?

Linnea picked out a few sweaters with stains, some jeans that didn't fit, and a broken doll that used to talk. She put the items in a bag and took them to her mom.

Oddly, she still didn't feel good about her decision. Linnea knew she would have been disappointed if someone had given that bag to *her*.

DECISION 2:

Linnea knew it would be wrong to give Aiysha a pile of junk, so she decided to compromise. She picked out a few beautiful outfits and a few broken toys. Toys, after all, mattered much more to Linnea than clothes, so a few good outfits wouldn't be missed.

She put everything in a bag and took it to her mom.

Her mom sorted through the bag then asked, "Linnea, do you think Jesus would have picked these things out for Aiysha?"

Linnea didn't like the question because she knew the answer was no.

DECISION 3:

Linnea considered giving Aiysha a few unimportant things, but she knew deep in her heart that Jesus wouldn't have made that decision.

She stood for a long time in her closet, staring at her clothes and toys.

With tears in her eyes, she picked out some of her very favorite things.

She didn't cry because of what she was losing—she cried because of what her friend had lost. It would be much easier to give up a few favorite things than to be like Aiysha and lose it all.

WHY DOES IT MATTER?

When we truly understand what Jesus has done for us—taking our punishment by dying on the cross—we'll want to be generous with others.

It's impossible to be like Christ and still be stingy.

In Acts 20:35 Jesus says, "We are more happy when we give than when we receive."

God calls us to live sacrificially. This means giving our time, money, compassion, and possessions to somebody who has a need. This also means giving the best of what we have, not just the leftovers.

Jesus set the perfect example!

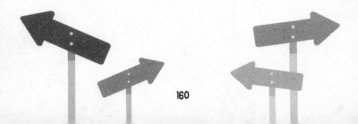

TWENTY-SIX

THE STILL, SMALL VOICE

The day of the wrestling tournament had arrived, and Levi knew there was a chance he could get first place. He had trained hard and practiced every afternoon. He was ready to do his best and bring home the golden trophy.

Winning was looking more likely as the day went on.

That all changed when he learned that his final opponent would be a girl named Violet.

Violet was a good athlete and a worthy competitor, but Levi had always been taught to treat young ladies with respect. And he didn't believe being aggressive toward a girl—even while wrestling—was the right decision.

It wasn't that girls were weak or unworthy—quite the opposite.

He had been taught to value them and treat them better than boys.

Not everyone shared Levi's conviction—in fact, other kids often laughed at him for refusing to wrestle girls—but he still believed that he shouldn't do it.

Levi's coach, as well as all the fans, wanted him to

go for it. But his conscience was telling him not to, and he knew he should follow his conscience.

Levi had only a few seconds to decide. Should he wrestle Violet and possibly win? Or should he just forfeit?

If you were Levi, what would you do?

Decision 1: Wrestle Violet. Times have changed and people are okay with boys wrestling girls now. (turn to page 163)

Decision 2: Make an exception this one time. Beating Violet would mean taking home the first-place trophy. (turn to page 164)

Decision 3: Stick to your conviction and forfeit the match. (turn to page 165)

DECISION 1:

Levi didn't want to wrestle Violet, but he also didn't want to forfeit the match. So he decided to wrestle. As he walked to the mat, his friends and teammates began cheering in the stands.

But it felt wrong.

The referee signaled the timekeeper, blew his whistle, and called, "Wrestle!"

But Levi was distracted the whole time.

Not only did he wrestle poorly and lose the match, but he lost his chance to explain to his teammates what he believed. He regretted the whole decision.

DECISION 2:

Levi wasn't willing to change his conviction, but he decided to make an exception this one time. He wanted the first-place trophy more than *anything*.

During the match, Levi accidentally hurt Violet during a takedown.

He felt terrible, especially when Violet and her coach falsely claimed he did it on purpose.

Levi won the trophy, but it didn't mean as much to him now.

He began to think it would have felt better to follow his conscience than to win.

DECISION 3:

Levi hated the idea of losing, but he hated the idea of ignoring his conscience even more.

He quickly prayed, asking God to give him peace about his decision. When he opened his eyes, he knew exactly what he should do.

He walked onto the mat and forfeited. After thanking Violet for being willing to compete, he returned to his spot on the sideline.

The crowd booed and his coach shook his head in disappointment, but Levi knew without a doubt that he was making the right decision. And that felt much better than winning.

WHY DOES IT MATTER?

Our conscience is the God-given inner voice that helps us decide between right and wrong.

Luke, the author of Acts, recorded the apostle Paul saying, "I always try to live so my own heart tells me I am not guilty before God or man" (Acts 24:16). We should try our best to do the same.

Sometimes, this means making decisions that other people don't understand. That's okay. It's always a sin whenever we choose to do something our conscience tells us is wrong. We ultimately answer to God, not to man, about how we respond to our conscience.

TWENTY-SEVEN

RAISE YOUR HAND!

Aurora was not ashamed of being a Christian. Far from it.

She loved going to church and talking about the Bible with her friends. She had even started a Bible study with some of the girls from her Sunday school class.

But sometimes she was too nervous to talk about Jesus with people who didn't know Him yet. She didn't want to make people feel uncomfortable, and she didn't want to be laughed at. So she just avoided saying anything about God.

One day her teacher was talking about religion. Aurora knew her teacher didn't believe in God, so she often prayed that he would come to know Christ.

The teacher asked, "Who in this classroom believes in the God of the Bible?"

Aurora looked around. She knew some of her friends believed in God, but they weren't raising their hands. It took courage to admit it publicly.

She wondered what would happen if she were the only student in the room to raise her hand.

What if my teacher laughs at me? What if I get a bad

grade? What if my friends stop talking to me?

She wondered if it would be smarter not to admit her love for Jesus in this situation.

Aurora knew she needed to decide. . .and fast.

If you were Aurora, what would you do?

Decision 1: Don't raise your hand. Why draw unwanted attention? (turn to page 169)

Decision 2: Wait to see if anyone else raises a hand. If not, don't be the only one. (turn to page 170)

Decision 3: Raise your hand. (turn to page 171)

DECISION 1:

Aurora kept her hand in her lap. She knew in her heart that she should raise it—regardless of what the rest of the class did—but she was scared. She didn't like attention, not even *good* attention.

As the teacher began speaking poorly of God, Aurora realized she had made a mistake. God had done so much for her, and she had been unwilling to do something small for Him.

She wished she could go back and change her decision.

DECISION 2:

Aurora waited to see what her classmates would do. When nobody budged, she kept her hand down as well.

"Hey," one of her classmates called from the back. "Don't you go to church?"

Aurora turned to see William talking to her. Now the entire class was watching.

"Yes," she said.

"Then why didn't you raise your hand?" William asked.

Aurora wished she had a good answer. She knew she should have raised her hand. She had invited many of her classmates to come to church, and now she had probably confused them by not being honest.

DECISION 3:

Aurora felt her heartbeat quicken and her throat tighten as she silently prayed.

She lifted her hand.

Her teacher looked at her for a moment and then said to the class, "At least we have one honest student in this classroom. Does no one else believe in the God of the Bible?"

A few more students raised their hands as well.

Aurora watched, grateful God had given her the courage to lead the way.

She knew she would never regret being honest with others about her faith in God.

WHY DOES IT MATTER?

Sometimes taking a stand for Christ or admitting to someone that we love God can feel scary. The world is filled with people who oppose God.

But God promises to always give us courage to stand strong in our faith.

Even better, He tells us we will never be alone—"Have I not told you? Be strong and have strength of heart! Do not be afraid or lose faith. For the Lord your God is with you anywhere you go" (Joshua 1:9).

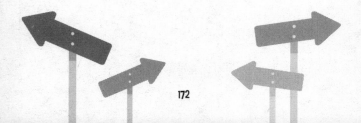

Twenty-Eight

LISTEN CAREFULLY

Leo couldn't sleep. He couldn't eat. He couldn't concentrate on his work.

All he could think about was the day before, when he had lied to his dad about something dumb. The lie had slipped out before he could think about it. And now he couldn't stop wondering why he had done it.

Even though his dad didn't know about the lie, Leo still felt sick about it.

The longer it bothered him, the more he wished he had just gotten caught and received a punishment. Being grounded from television or games this weekend seemed better than the guilt he was feeling.

I wish this terrible feeling would just go away!

He tried to forget about it and just move on, but he couldn't.

Leo thought getting away with a lie would make him feel better—happy, even—but his conscience wouldn't let him forget it. Every time he thought about his dad, he felt sick to his stomach.

He knew his conscience was the Holy Spirit's way of convicting him of sin.

He also knew he needed to listen to the Holy Spirit and respond the right way.

But his dad had no idea about the lie, so why would Leo ruin everything by telling him? His dad would be very disappointed.

If you were Leo, what would you do?

Decision 1: Go to Dad and tell him what happened. Confess the lie and ask for forgiveness. (turn to page 175)

Decision 2: Stay quiet and hope the awful feeling passes soon. (turn to page 176)

Decision 3: Confess the lie to God and then do something nice for Dad to make things up to him. (turn to page 177)

DECISION 1:

Leo was sitting on the couch when his dad came home from work. As soon as he walked through the front door, Leo took a deep breath and said, "Dad, can we talk?"

Leo confessed everything. He told his dad about the lie, explained how he had been unable to sleep, eat, or concentrate as a result, and asked for forgiveness. He also explained that he was willing to take whatever punishment his dad planned to give him.

Instead of being angry, Leo's dad pulled him into a hug and thanked him.

"I think you've suffered enough this time," his dad said. "Thank you for telling me the truth."

DECISION 2:

As much as Leo wanted to confess everything and ask for forgiveness, he couldn't risk disappointing his dad. He knew his dad hated lying more than anything.

So Leo stayed quiet, hoping the awful feeling passed soon.

But it didn't. A week later, Leo was still troubled. And now he was making other mistakes because he was tired, hungry, and struggling in school.

He began to wonder if it would have just been easier to come clean days ago.

DECISION 3:

Leo knew he had sinned when he lied, but he didn't want to tell his dad about it.

So he prayed, asking God to forgive him.

And then he decided to do something nice for his dad, hoping that would ease his conscience.

He mowed the yard, took out the trash, and washed the car without being told.

And he still felt miserable.

He began to think the only way he could move on would be to finally tell his dad the truth.

WHY DOES IT MATTER?

Part of living a Christian life is being honest and regularly asking for forgiveness when we sin. Having the humility to do so is extremely hard, but it's essential for our growth.

Whenever we sin against someone, we have the responsibility to go to that person and ask for forgiveness.

James 5:16 says, "Tell your sins to each other. And pray for each other so you may be healed."

It isn't easy, but it's the right thing to do.

Thankfully, God is always willing to help us do what is right.

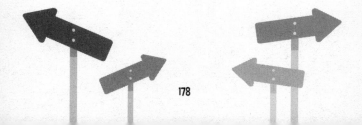

Twenty-Nine

BIG DEAL

Anna was allowed to play with the neighborhood kids at the ball field near their house, but her parents had one rule: as soon as it was dark enough for the lights to turn on, she had to come home.

Every afternoon when Anna headed out to play, her parents would remind her. As soon as the lights came on, she was to stop whatever she was doing and say goodbye.

Even if she didn't want to leave.

Even if her friends begged her to stay.

Even if the rule didn't make sense.

Most of the time it wasn't a problem. Anna's friends knew her parents' rule, and they helped remind her.

One evening they were playing a game of kickball, and it was almost Anna's turn to kick. With only one person ahead of her and two already on base, she knew she had a good chance to bring them home.

But then the lights popped on.

She groaned. The bases were loaded, and she could hear her teammates cheering for her from the sidelines.

How could she quit now?

She knew the right thing to do would be to obey her parents and wave goodbye, but her friends really wanted her to kick the ball. What if she went home and her friends didn't invite her to play next time? Besides, she could kick the ball quickly and then head home. Her parents would never know.

If you were Anna, what would you do?

Decision 1: Finish your turn and then head home. It would be selfish to let the entire team down. (turn to page 181)

Decision 2: Pretend not to notice the light. Sometimes apologizing is better than asking permission. (turn to page 182)

Decision 3: Obey immediately, even if it disappoints the other kids. (turn to page 183)

DECISION 1:

Anna decided to finish her turn and then head home. After all, wouldn't it be wrong to let down her entire team? She didn't want to be selfish.

The pitcher rolled the ball toward home plate, and Anna kicked it as hard as she could. The ball sailed far into the outfield as her teammates began running the bases.

But instead of cheering, her teammates on the sideline quietly pointed to the opposite side of the field.

Anna turned to see her dad walking toward her.

Immediately, she regretted her decision.

DECISION 2:

Anna decided to ignore the lights. Who could prove she had seen them?

If anyone asked, she could simply act surprised and then apologize.

"Hey, the lights just came on!" the pitcher yelled.

Anna shrugged. She wished he hadn't said that.

"Aren't you supposed to head home?" the pitcher asked.

Anna shrugged again.

Another one of her teammates called out, "Aren't you always talking about the Bible and how kids are supposed to obey their parents?"

Anna knew they were right. She had missed an opportunity to show her friends what it looked like to obey God.

DECISION 3:

Anna wanted to stay and finish the game, but she knew obeying her parents was more important.

"Come on, Anna!" one of her teammates yelled from the field. "Just kick the ball!"

"I'm sorry, but I can't!" Anna said. "You know the rule."

"Big deal!" another teammate laughed.

Anna waved politely and turned to run off the field.

And that's when she saw him. Her dad was walking toward her, a big smile on his face.

She had no idea her dad would see her decision, but she was thankful he had. And even better, God had seen her too.

183

WHY DOES IT MATTER?

God delights in our obedience. It's one of the greatest ways we show our love for Him. Did you know 1 Samuel 15:22 says God would rather have obedience than sacrifices? Obedience is that important to Him.

One of the ways we obey God is by obeying our parents. Unless our parents ask us to sin, we have a responsibility to obey.

"Children, as Christians, obey your parents. This is the right thing to do" (Ephesians 6:1).

Obedience may not always be fun, but it's always right.

And God rewards what is right.

THIRTY

JUST DO IT!

Mason loved Saturdays. After a long week of school, homework, and sports practice, all he could think about was relaxing. He loved spending his Saturdays sleeping late, lying around, and playing games.

His mom would bring him snacks and lunch, and he didn't have to do anything he didn't want to.

The worst part of Saturday was when it ended.

One day, as Mason was lying on the couch surfing channels on the television, he noticed how hard his mom was working. She was cleaning the kitchen, making meals, doing the laundry, and vacuuming the floors. All while Mason did nothing.

He wondered why he had never noticed this before. His Saturdays were work-free, but his mom's work was never done.

Has it always been this way? He guessed the answer was yes. Moms work very hard.

He knew it wasn't fair to make his mom do all the work by herself, but he also didn't want to give up his easy Saturday.

He wondered if, instead of lying on the couch, he

should offer to help his mom. It would make her Saturday easier, and he could still enjoy part of his weekend when the work was done.

If you were Mason, what would you do?

Decision 1: Pretend not to notice Mom working so hard. She's the adult, so the housework is her job. (turn to page 187)

Decision 2: Thank Mom for all she does for you. (turn to page 188)

Decision 3: Turn off the television and offer to help. (turn to page 189)

DECISION 1:

Mason hated that his mom worked so hard, but he also didn't want to give up his lazy Saturdays. So he pretended not to notice her. He knew he would one day become an adult, and he would help around the house then.

He settled back on the pillows and continued channel surfing.

Too bad his mom couldn't enjoy being a kid again.

DECISION 2:

Mason wasn't ready to give up his lazy day, but he also felt bad for his mom. So whenever she walked through the living room, he thanked her several times.

Not taking his eyes off the screen, he would say, "Thank you, Mom!" every time he saw her carrying a stack of freshly folded laundry or a set of clean sheets for his bed.

But the words felt empty.

He knew that putting feet to his words would be the best way to thank her.

Unfortunately, he didn't want to put feet to anything. It was Saturday.

DECISION 3:

Mason wanted to keep watching television, but he knew his mom probably wanted a break too. She worked hard to care for him, and he felt wrong doing nothing on Saturdays while she did everything.

Despite what he wanted to do, he turned off the television and walked into the kitchen.

"How can I help you, Mom?" he asked.

He was shocked by the look of surprise and love that his mom gave him.

He loved his mom very much, and he was glad she knew it by how he acted.

WHY DOES IT MATTER?

First John 3:18 says, "My children, let us not love with words or in talk only. Let us love by what we do and in truth."

Throughout the Bible, God tells us that what we do is more important than what we say.

It isn't enough to say we love someone if our actions don't back it up.

One of the greatest ways we can show our families that we love them is by serving them at home whenever and however we can.

Does your family know you love them? If not, don't just say it with your words, but show it with your actions too.

THiRTY-ONE

SCREEN TEST

Claire and her friends met outside the movie theater on a Friday night to eat pizza and watch the new movie for kids. Claire had looked forward to this day all week, and she was excited that her parents had trusted her to make good choices on her own.

She and her friends walked into the theater and started ordering food, when one of her friends, Molly, whispered in her ear, "We're not actually here to watch the new movie."

Claire looked at her, confused. "What do you mean?" she asked.

"We're going to watch something else." Molly pointed across the theater to large posters that advertised a different movie. Claire could tell the movie wasn't meant for kids her age, and it was filled with scenes and language that didn't please God.

She knew her parents—and, more importantly, God—would be disappointed by this deception.

"But I thought we were here to see this movie!" she said, pointing back to the movie poster she recognized.

Her friend laughed. "That movie is for babies," she

said. "We just wanted our parents to think that's why we're here."

By this time, Claire's other friends had gathered around, pizza in hand. She realized she had been the only one who didn't know about the plan. Either her friends didn't trust her to keep a secret, or they knew she would think it was wrong.

"Let's go," Molly said, leading the group of girls toward the movie room.

If you were Claire, what would you do?

Decision 1: Say you aren't feeling well and need to go home. (turn to page 193)

Decision 2: Tell your friends that they shouldn't go to a movie that their parents haven't approved. (turn to page 194)

Decision 3: Go to the movie with your friends and hope it isn't that bad. (turn to page 195)

DECISION 1:

Claire's friends stopped to look at her. Her mind raced. She didn't want to watch the movie, but she also didn't want to upset her friends.

"My stomach hurts," she said. "I think I need to go home."

"Is it because you don't want to see this movie?" Molly asked.

"Of course not!" Claire said, laughing. "I really wish I could go. See you guys on Monday!"

She turned and left the theater.

She was glad she had avoided watching the movie, but she was also sad about not telling the truth. She had a feeling they knew she was lying, which just made her feel worse.

DECISION 2:

Claire took a deep breath. "Guys, we told our parents we were watching *this* movie." She pointed to the poster in front of them. "It'd be wrong to sneak in to another one, and it'd especially be wrong to see a movie we shouldn't watch."

Molly rolled her eyes. "I knew you'd be the one to ruin it."

The words stung a little, but Claire realized it was actually a compliment.

If her friends were going to be deceptive, she had no problem with being the friend who ruined their plans.

As they walked toward the correct movie room, Claire noticed that a few of the girls looked relieved.

DECISION 3:

Claire didn't want to see the movie, but she also didn't want to upset her friends, so she shrugged and followed Molly. She hoped the movie wasn't as bad as she thought it would be—and she definitely hoped her parents wouldn't ask her about it later.

The movie was *terrible*! If only Claire had stood up to her friends or at least left the theater. . . .

Now, in addition to the guilt she felt, she was stuck remembering the awful things she had seen.

She had missed an important opportunity to do right.

WHY DOES IT MATTER?

Temptation isn't a sin. We know this to be true because Jesus "was tempted in every way we are tempted, but He did not sin" (Hebrews 4:15).

Sin happens when we give in to temptation, and we usually give in only after we convince ourselves that the sin will bring us happiness.

Sin may make us happy for a moment, but it always brings destruction in the end. Sin ruins relationships, hurts our conscience, and steals our joy.

Thankfully, God always provides us with an alternative to sin—obedience. And He promises to help us at every step.

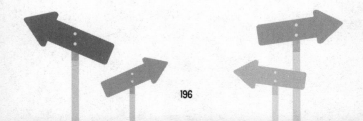

THIRTY-TWO

FOR HEAVEN'S SAKE

Titan loved Jesus and wanted his friends at school to love Jesus too.

He took every chance he had to share his faith and his love for God, and he always invited his friends to church. He didn't mind the fact that he had the reputation at school of being "the Christian kid." Several of his friends called him "Preacher," and he actually liked it.

He *wanted* to be a pastor someday.

However, one of his classmates, Hunter, didn't believe in Jesus. During lunch one day Hunter said to him, "Titan, do you believe I'm going to hell someday?"

Hunter's friends turned to see how Titan would answer.

Titan had been asked many questions about his beliefs, but this question was truly the hardest. He didn't like saying or doing things that made his friends uncomfortable. But he also didn't want to lie.

Titan was faced with a tough choice.

It would be much easier to laugh and say, "No! Of course not! You're going to heaven." Hunter would probably be happy with this answer.

But Titan had memorized John 14:6, where Jesus says, "I am the Way and the Truth and the Life. No one can go to the Father except by Me." So Titan knew it could actually hurt Hunter in the end if he didn't believe trusting Jesus was necessary for salvation.

Titan didn't want to be responsible for helping Hunter go to hell.

Hunter and his friends were waiting for an answer, and Titan knew he needed to say something.

If you were Titan, what would you do?

Decision 1: Change the subject and talk about something that wouldn't hurt Hunter's feelings. (turn to page 199)
Decision 2: Tell Hunter publicly that he is going to heaven, but tell him privately that he needs to trust Jesus. (turn to page 200)
Decision 3: Tell Hunter the truth that faith in Jesus is required for salvation. (turn to page 201)

DECISION 1:

Titan smiled at Hunter and said, "Did you see the end of that baseball game last night? Impressive, right?"

Hunter shrugged and kept staring at Titan, but Titan wouldn't take the bait.

He was determined to avoid hurting Hunter's feelings.

Titan never did answer the question. A couple weeks later, Hunter and his family moved to a new city and school, and Titan wondered if he'd ever see him again. Maybe someone would have enough courage to tell Hunter the truth about salvation through Jesus before it was too late.

DECISION 2:

Titan smiled. "Of course you're going to heaven," he said. "How could someone as nice and fun as you end up in hell?"

But as soon as the words left his mouth, he knew he had done something terribly wrong. Giving someone the assurance of heaven when he is going to hell isn't love at all.

On the way out of the lunchroom, Titan tapped Hunter on the shoulder. "Hey, about that question," he said. "You know you need to trust in Jesus, right?"

But Hunter ignored him. He had moved on to talking to his friends about baseball.

DECISION 3:

Titan wanted to tell Hunter that he was going to heaven, but he knew he didn't have the right to give him false assurance of his salvation.

What would Jesus do?

Titan thought about the times Jesus had responded to hard questions by quoting the Bible, so Hunter decided to quote a verse he had learned in kids club at church.

"If you say with your mouth that Jesus is Lord, and believe in your heart that God raised Him from the dead, you will be saved from the punishment of sin" (Romans 10:9).

"We should talk about that sometime," Hunter said.

And Titan agreed.

WHY DOES IT MATTER?

The Gospel is offensive to those who don't believe it.

In 1 Corinthians 1:23 Paul says, "We preach that Christ died on a cross to save them from their sins. These words are hard for the Jews to listen to. The Greek people think it is foolish."

And it's no different in our world today.

People who hear that faith in Christ is required for salvation often believe it is "hard to listen to" or even "foolish," just as they did during Bible times. But this doesn't eliminate our responsibility to tell people the truth.

Our honesty matters more than their comfort.

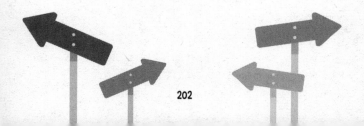

THIRTY-THREE

WANT TO KNOW A SECRET?

One day Evie invited her best friend, Ruby, over to her house to play. They loved flipping through books, fixing each other's hair, and telling each other all about their day.

Evie loved that they could tell each other *anything*.

As they were sitting in Evie's room, Ruby said, "Evie, I have a secret to tell you. Can you promise you won't ever tell anyone?"

"Of course!" Evie agreed.

Ruby was the kind of friend she had always wanted, and Evie loved her enough to protect their friendship at all costs. She would never spread any of her secrets.

Ruby whispered the secret into Evie's ear.

Immediately, Evie regretted making the promise. The secret was actually something that could hurt Ruby.

Evie knew she should tell Ruby's parents. Her friend was in danger, and Evie didn't want her to get hurt.

But she had promised not to tell! If she spilled Ruby's secret—especially to Ruby's parents—their friendship might be ruined forever.

If you were Evie, what would you do?

Decision 1: Don't tell anyone. Promises should always be kept. (turn to page 205)

Decision 2: Tell Ruby's parents right away. (turn to page 206)

Decision 3: Explain to Ruby that she should go with you to get help from either her parents or yours. (turn to page 207)

DECISION 1:

Evie knew she should get help for Ruby, but she also didn't want to hurt such a good friendship. Even more, she hated the thought of breaking her promise. *Breaking a promise is the same as lying, isn't it?*

So she kept her promise.

It didn't take long for her to realize this was a terrible mistake.

Not only did Ruby's secret hurt her, but in time, it eventually destroyed their friendship as well. Evie wished she had gotten help right away.

DECISION 2:

Evie knew Ruby trusted her, but she also knew she couldn't keep the secret to herself if she wanted to protect Ruby. So she stood up, told Ruby she was going to the kitchen to get snacks, and ran right to the phone.

She called Ruby's mom and told her everything.

Ruby's mom thanked her and said she would be there soon.

When Evie hung up, she turned to see Ruby standing in the doorway of the kitchen.

She knew immediately that their friendship was over.

She wondered if there could have possibly been a better way to handle it.

DECISION 3:

For a moment, Evie sat next to Ruby and thought about her options. She loved Ruby too much to either keep the secret or spill it behind her back.

There had to be another way.

"Ruby," she finally said, her eyes filling with tears, "this isn't a secret you should keep. I think we should go to someone and get help together. Would you rather go to your parents or mine?"

At first, Ruby was silent, and Evie wondered if their friendship was ruined. But then Ruby said, "Let's go to your parents."

Evie could tell Ruby was glad they were going to get help from someone who loved them.

WHY DOES IT MATTER?

Secrets are fun to tell, but sometimes they're dangerous to keep.

When we hear a secret that shouldn't be kept, we should never put our friends in danger by keeping quiet.

As Christians, being a good friend doesn't always mean doing what our friends want—it means doing what they *need*. It's always important to have a friend who will tell us the truth when necessary.

"The pains given by a friend are faithful, but the kisses of one who hates you are false" (Proverbs 27:6).

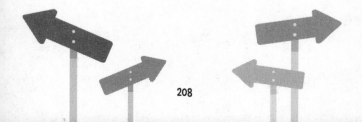

THIRTY-FOUR

A TRUTH WORTH OVER
THREE HUNDRED DOLLARS

Cyrus had two older brothers whom he loved very much. But what he didn't love was having to wear their hand-me-down clothes all the time. He never got to wear anything new.

While Cyrus's friends were getting new jackets or sweatshirts, Cyrus was always wearing the same clothes his brothers had worn for years before.

It was so obvious his clothes were passed down that his nickname at school was "Little Brother."

What Cyrus wanted most in the whole world was a pair of leather sneakers that all his friends were wearing. The shoes were white with green stripes and a zipper on the side. And they were brand-new. No one would ever mistake those for hand-me-downs.

If only Cyrus could have them. . . .

I'd never ask for anything ever again!

According to his friends, the sneakers cost three hundred dollars. Cyrus's parents worked very hard to provide for him and his siblings; three hundred dollars was just too much to spend on a pair of sneakers that he would soon outgrow.

But he wanted them.

If you were Cyrus, what would you do?

Decision 1: Learn to be content without the shoes. They're too expensive. (turn to page 211)

Decision 2: Tell Mom and Dad that those sneakers are the only way you could ever be happy. (turn to page 212)

Decision 3: Ruin all your other shoes so your parents will have to buy new ones. (turn to page 213)

DECISION 1:

Cyrus loved the leather sneakers, but he knew his feet would grow out of them soon enough. Even more, he didn't want to ask his parents to spend their hard-earned money on something he didn't need.

His closet was already filled with shoes—even if they weren't white with green stripes and a zipper on the side.

He prayed, asking God to help him "be happy with whatever I have" (Philippians 4:11). Contentment, he realized, would be more valuable to him in life than any pair of sneakers.

DECISION 2:

Cyrus tried—and failed—to forget about the sneakers. Finally, he decided to tell his parents the truth.

"Mom and Dad," he said one evening, "those leather sneakers are the only way I could ever be happy."

He saw his mom trying not to smile, and it made him angry. Obviously, his mom had never been a kid!

"Son," his dad said, "we're not buying the sneakers. I'm sorry."

It was in that moment that Cyrus realized he would live a life without happiness.

DECISION 3:

Cyrus knew if he asked his parents for the sneakers, they would say no because his closet was filled with wearable shoes.

So he crafted a plan.

After school one day, he sneaked into his room with a knife and cut huge holes in all his shoes. Now his parents would have to buy him the leather sneakers.

Except they didn't. And since he had destroyed his shoes on purpose, Cyrus's parents made him wear them to school and church anyway, even with the ugly holes.

Not only did Cyrus's plan fail, but his shoes now looked worse than ever. He should have been content with what he had been given.

WHY DOES IT MATTER?

Contentment is a hard skill to learn, but it's necessary if we want to be like Jesus.

When Paul says in Philippians 4:13, "I can do all things because Christ gives me the strength," he is talking specifically about contentment.

God promises to give us strength to be content with whatever situation we're experiencing. Isn't that an amazing promise?

Whether or not we have the perfect clothes, toys, friends, or life, God still gives us everything we need to be content. That's a promise that's worth far more than any three-hundred-dollar leather sneakers!

THIRTY-FIVE

A MAP TO YOUR OWN BURIED TREASURE

Avy loved to read. She went to the library every week and picked out the greatest books she could find. She was definitely the best reader in her class.

Someday, Avy hoped, reading would help her become a leader.

Her parents told her she would make a great leader as long as she chose to do right.

There was just one problem. Between all her textbooks, library books, and the books she owned, Avy rarely had time to read her Bible!

This reality bothered her because her Sunday school teacher was always talking about how important it is for God's children to read His Word.

During Sunday school one week, Avy's teacher read Psalm 119:11, which says, "Your Word have I hid in my heart, that I may not sin against You."

But Avy knew she wasn't hiding God's Word in her heart. She loved talking about the Bible, but she hardly ever read it.

She knew the Bible taught how to live and grow

closer to God. But, if she were to be honest, she would rather read her other books.

They were easier to understand.

If you were Avy, what would you do?

Decision 1: Keep reading whatever books you want. Lots of Christians don't read their Bibles. (turn to page 217)

Decision 2: Read some Christian books so that reading the Bible will be unnecessary. (turn to page 218)

Decision 3: Find a way to spend at least a few minutes every day reading the Bible without interruption. (turn to page 219)

DECISION 1:

Avy knew she should probably start reading her Bible every day, but she also knew many Christians who didn't read their Bibles very often.

If it isn't important to them, why should it be important to me?

Avy continued reading library books, hoping her Sunday school teacher would tell her everything about the Bible that she needed to know.

Unfortunately, this meant Avy would never become the best Christian leader she could be.

DECISION 2:

Even though Avy knew she should learn more about God by reading her Bible, she decided to read fun books by Christian authors instead.

She learned many good things as she read, growing in her faith and becoming a stronger leader.

But she always felt like something was missing. She knew she should read her Bible every day—in addition to Christian books—but she didn't know where to start. It would also require some work on her part.

Shouldn't reading always be just for fun?

DECISION 3:

Avy knew she could afford to spend a few minutes every day reading God's Word. It wouldn't always be easy to understand, and she suspected it wouldn't always be as fun as reading a library book.

But she knew it was the most important reading she could do.

And she was right.

Every morning she started her day by reading the Bible. Very quickly she learned to love these few minutes she spent with God. And soon she realized she was learning far more about God than she ever thought possible!

Over time, the Bible became her favorite book.

WHY DOES IT MATTER?

Can you imagine if someone told you where you could find your own buried treasure—even giving you a map and offering to help you find it—and you said you were too busy?

How foolish that would be!

And yet God has given us the greatest treasure of all in the pages of His Word, but we often fail to spend time reading it.

Proverbs 3:14 says that getting wisdom is "better than getting silver and fine gold."

And how do we get wisdom? By spending time in God's Word.

Go look for your own buried treasure!

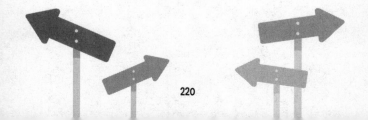

THiRTY-Six

SOMETHING TO TALK ABOUT

Micah's family loved God and worshipped Him every week at church, but his grandpa wanted nothing to do with Jesus.

In fact, Micah's grandpa told everyone in the family that he didn't want them to share the Gospel with him ever again. He was tired of hearing about God!

He even announced he would never again talk to anybody who discussed religion with him.

The family was saddened by this news. They prayed God would change his heart, but they also honored his wishes and stopped inviting him to church.

One day, Micah's grandpa learned he was very sick and didn't have long to live. Micah knew that the most important thing his grandpa needed to do before he died was trust Jesus as his personal Savior. He also knew that talking to his grandpa about salvation could be disastrous. His grandpa might get angry and say hurtful things. And Micah didn't want that to be their last memory together.

But he didn't want him to spend an eternity apart from Jesus either.

One afternoon, Micah's grandpa invited him to his house. Micah knew this was his chance. If he was going to share the Gospel with his grandpa, it was now or never.

If you were Micah, what would you do?

Decision 1: Let somebody else have the hard conversation with Grandpa. (turn to page 223)

Decision 2: Honor Grandpa's wishes and don't talk about Jesus. Grandpa is responsible for his own choices. (turn to page 224)

Decision 3: Take the opportunity to talk to Grandpa about his need to trust Jesus. (turn to page 225)

DECISION 1:

Micah loved his grandpa, but he didn't want their final conversation to end in a fight. So he decided to let someone else tell him about the Gospel.

Micah sat with his grandpa, discussing everything from cars and baseball to school and friends. The entire time they talked, Micah couldn't shake the feeling that they should be discussing something far more important.

He hoped someone would have the courage to talk to Grandpa before it was too late.

DECISION 2:

Micah desperately wanted to talk to his grandpa about Jesus, but he decided to honor his grandpa's wish. Micah decided Grandpa alone was responsible for his own choices. He hated the thought that his grandpa could end up in hell, but what choice did Micah have?

Later that night when he heard that his grandpa had died, he suddenly wished he had been brave enough to have the conversation, even if it had upset his grandpa.

DECISION 3:

Micah didn't want to anger his grandpa, but he knew it was far more important for his grandpa to hear the truth than to merely have a comfortable conversation. . . especially if he was about to face God.

Micah opened his Bible and sat down next to his grandfather.

"Can we talk?" Micah asked.

"Of course," his grandpa said. "We can talk about anything."

As carefully and clearly as he could, Micah shared the good news of the Gospel with his grandpa. And he was shocked that his grandpa listened to every word.

He was thankful he had taken the chance.

WHY DOES IT MATTER?

As children of God, we have the privilege and responsibility of telling others about Jesus.

People will often listen to kids, even when they're unwilling to listen to other adults! So, as a kid, you have a unique opportunity to share the Gospel with your family.

Ask God for courage to have these conversations with people who need to hear the truth.

First Peter 3:15 says, "Always be ready to tell everyone who asks you why you believe as you do. Be gentle as you speak and show respect."

Thirty-Seven

KEEP IT IN THE FAMILY

Cora was great at getting along with people and making them feel good. She always knew how to encourage her friends or compliment her teachers. She could even get along with people who were harder to befriend. Everyone wanted to be friends with Cora.

But Cora had one major weakness.

She struggled at being kind to her family at home.

She was kind and loving with her friends, but when she was with her family, she was mean and selfish. She didn't care about getting along with her siblings. And her parents were often the victims of her bad moods.

One day Cora's sister kindly asked her, "Why do you care more about being nice to everyone at school or church than you do your own family?"

The words stung. Cora had never really considered how odd her behavior was. Maybe it was because she and her family naturally loved each other, so she never felt the need to treat them kindly.

Cora opened her mouth, ready to remind her sister of all the ways *she* had failed too.

But something in her heart made her pause.

If you were Cora, what would you do?

Decision 1: Continue treating your family however you want. They'll love you no matter what. (turn to page 229)

Decision 2: Pretend to be in a good mood all the time. (turn to page 230)

Decision 3: Ask your family to forgive you, and then ask God to help you love and serve your family with a better attitude. (turn to page 231)

DECISION 1:

Cora laughed at her sister. "How can *you* say that?" Cora said. "You have your own bad habits and moods too."

Cora knew her family would love her no matter how she acted. That's what families are for, right? Her sister needed to mind her own business.

Strangely, none of these thoughts made Cora feel any better.

Did the rest of her family feel the same way as her sister?

If so, she wasn't sure how to fix it.

DECISION 2:

Cora didn't want to be seen as the one who was always in a bad mood, so she decided to fix it. From now on, she would always be in a good mood—or at least she would fake it. She would paste a cheerful smile on her face every day and only say things that made her family happy.

Except it didn't take long for Cora to realize how exhausting this was.

Being fake took a lot of work, and she actually felt more upset than before.

There has to be a better idea!

DECISION 3:

Cora was tempted to tell her sister to just go away, but she knew her sister was right.

Cora felt terrible that she had treated her family so poorly.

That night at supper, Cora asked her family to forgive her for how she had been acting. She also asked God to help her love and serve her family.

Soon Cora realized it was far easier to just be kind to others. Her mood even began to improve as she thought about ways she could help the people she loved!

WHY DOES IT MATTER?

Sometimes the people we know and love the most are the ones we treat with the most disrespect. This behavior is unfortunate and should never characterize the life of a Christ follower.

In John 15:12, Jesus says, "This is what I tell you to do: Love each other just as I have loved you."

God isn't pleased when we are unloving to anyone, but He especially wants us to be loving to our families.

Ephesians 6:2 says, "Respect your father and mother. This is the first Law given that had a promise."

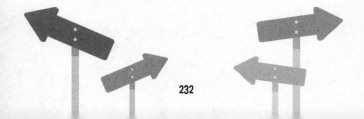

THIRTY-EIGHT

HOW (NOT) TO MAKE FRIENDS

Josiah wanted friends, but he also wanted to be respected.

He liked the idea of making people nervous by simply walking into a room. Even though Josiah knew he wasn't tough and strong at all, he liked pretending. And he loved how it felt when he fooled others.

One day at school, his classmate Christian handed out invitations to a birthday party, and Josiah was shocked. Nearly every kid in the class received an invitation, except for Josiah!

Why wouldn't Christian want me to be there? He knows I'm great at giving presents!

When school ended, Josiah sat in his chair, holding back tears. Crying, after all, wouldn't make him look tough.

His teacher sat next to him. "What's wrong?" she asked. Josiah explained how disappointed he was to be left out of the party. His teacher replied, "Is there a chance Christian doesn't know how much you want to be his friend? Sometimes acting tough makes people believe you don't care about them."

233

Josiah had never thought of that before. He thought his friends knew how much he cared for them. His teacher shared Proverbs 18:24: "A man who has friends must be a friend."

Josiah knew he needed to decide.

If you were Josiah, what would you do?

Decision 1: Quit caring about your classmates. If they don't want to be your friend, why should you want to be theirs? (turn to page 235)

Decision 2: Only be friendly with the kids who are friendly to you. (turn to page 236)

Decision 3: Stop trying to look tough and choose to be friendly to everyone. (turn to page 237)

DECISION 1:

Josiah decided once and for all to ignore his class-mates. If they didn't want to invite him to their birthday parties, he didn't want to go.

He acted even tougher and stronger than he did before.

But, strangely enough, this only made him feel sad-der and smaller. Nobody sat by him at lunch. Nobody played with him at recess. Nobody invited him over.

He couldn't live like this! He needed to make some changes.

He decided to talk to his teacher again and see what she suggested.

DECISION 2:

Josiah wasn't ready to completely change his tough, strong reputation at school, but he decided he should start being a little kinder. Maybe it wouldn't hurt to smile or say something friendly once in a while.

He decided he would start being friendly, but only to the kids who were friendly to him.

The problem? None of the kids were friendly to him anymore. In his desire to be respected, Josiah had accidentally pushed most of his classmates away.

If he ever wanted any friends, he would need to start from the very beginning.

DECISION 3:

Josiah decided that, if he wanted to be like Jesus, he needed to stop trying to act tough all the time. After all, Jesus was a loving friend to everyone He met.

Josiah also understood that he needed to be friendly in order to have friends. Waiting for people to be friendly to him first wouldn't work.

So he started being kind to everyone.

It didn't take long for kids to see the change, and Josiah was amazed at how soon he had friends again.

WHY DOES IT MATTER?

Good friends are valuable, improving life in every way. They share in our joys and disappointments, and we share in theirs. The very best friends also want us to honor God.

The number one way to find good friends is to *be* a good friend. Perhaps one of the greatest descriptions of a good friend is found in Romans 12:10 (CSB)—"Love one another deeply as brothers and sisters. Take the lead in honoring one another."

Be the type of friend you wish to have.

THIRTY-NINE

A MODEST PROPOSAL

Ivy's parents had very specific ideas about what she should wear and how she should look when she went to school. And for the most part, Ivy had no problem obeying their rules. She knew her parents loved her and wanted the best for her.

But when her friends started wearing makeup and shorter skirts, Ivy didn't want to stick out like a sore thumb. She wanted to fit in.

When Ivy asked her parents if she could start dressing like her friends and wearing makeup, they kindly explained why their answer was "No." One day, they told her, she could wear makeup, but she wasn't ready quite yet.

Ivy didn't like their decision.

She didn't want to be the only girl who still wore longer skirts and no makeup.

What will my friends think? What if my friends laugh at me behind my back?

Was wearing makeup really a big deal? What was the problem with shorter skirts?

If you were Ivy, what would you do?

Decision 1: Sneak makeup and clothes into your backpack and change once you get to school. Change back before you go home. (turn to page 241)

Decision 2: Follow the rules, explaining to your friends that obeying your parents is important to you. (turn to page 242)

Decision 3: Do what you want. It's your body and your choice. (turn to page 243)

DECISION 1:

Ivy didn't want to upset her parents, but she *did* want to look like her friends. So she crafted a plan. She would sneak makeup and clothes into her backpack and change in the bathroom at school. As long as she remembered to change back before heading home, she would make everyone happy.

Somehow, Ivy's decision didn't feel right, but she enjoyed blending in with her friends.

Her plan was working. . .until her mom came to get her for a dentist appointment Ivy had forgotten about.

The disappointment on her mom's face made her instantly regret her decision.

DECISION 2:

Ivy wanted to please her friends, but she wanted to please God and her parents far more. So at lunch, when her friends asked why she wasn't wearing makeup, she explained that her parents weren't ready for her to do that yet.

"Are you mad at them?" one of her friends asked.

"No," said Ivy. "Even though I don't understand, I trust they know what's best."

To her surprise, her friends didn't laugh at her. In fact, they told her she was fortunate to have parents who cared about her.

Ivy agreed.

DECISION 3:

Ivy was angry that her parents wouldn't let her make her own decisions. It was her body, after all, so it should be her choice. What did her parents understand about being a kid, anyway?

She decided she would do what she wanted to do. If she wanted to wear the short skirts and the makeup, she would. Her attitude broke her parents' heart, but she didn't care. She wanted freedom.

Except instead of feeling free, she felt *trapped*—trapped by unimportant opinions from people who didn't love her nearly as much as her parents did.

She wished she could take it all back.

WHY DOES IT MATTER?

Modesty is more than just the type of clothing we wear. Modesty is about the condition of our hearts. Whom do we want to glorify? With whom do we want to identify? Whose approval and attention do we seek?

First Peter 3:4 gives us a good definition of how God defines modesty—"Your beauty should come from the inside. It should come from the heart. This is the kind that lasts. Your beauty should be a gentle and quiet spirit. In God's sight this is of great worth and no amount of money can buy it."

FORTY

JUST DO SOMETHING

Steven wasn't sure how he wanted to spend his summer, but he did know he wanted to honor God. He had three choices:

First, his church was hosting a missions trip to Mexico. Steven loved the idea of learning about a new culture, meeting fellow Christians, and sharing the Gospel with kids at a Bible club.

Second, the local Christian camp was looking for kids who were willing to spend their weekends serving. The camp especially needed boys his age who could help mow lawns and clean up trash. Helping a camp reach kids for Christ sounded fantastic! He knew so many struggling kids who just needed to be encouraged in their walk with Christ.

Third, he had the opportunity to start a lawn-mowing business with his older brother. By mowing lawns in the community and getting paid, they could volunteer their time and do yard work for widows who couldn't afford to hire anyone. Steven knew caring for widows was an important part of being a Christian.

All three choices seemed like good ideas, but which one was best?

If you were Steven, what would you do?

Decision 1: Join the church's missions trip to Mexico. (turn to page 247)

Decision 2: Work for the local Christian camp. (turn to page 248)

Decision 3: Start a business to help widows in your church. (turn to page 249)

DECISION 1:

Steven decided to join his church's missions trip to Mexico. He spent two weeks learning about his fellow brothers and sisters in Christ who lived in Mexico, and he committed to praying for them regularly once he returned. He also shared the good news of the Gospel with kids at a Bible club. He loved telling others about Jesus, and the trip gave him a better understanding and appreciation for ministry around the world.

The trip changed his life in many wonderful ways, and he didn't regret it.

DECISION 2:

Steven decided to spend his summer weekends working for the local Christian camp. He loved serving the camp staff and meeting kids who wanted to strengthen their walk with God. He had many great discussions about the Gospel, and he even led a couple campers to Christ.

He also learned to work hard. He mowed lawns, cleaned up trash, and worked in the snack shop. By the end of the summer, he was tired!

But spending his weekends serving at camp changed his life in many wonderful ways, and he didn't regret it.

DECISION 3:

Steven decided to start a lawn-mowing business with his older brother.

Together, they spent the summer mowing lawns in the community and using their income and resources to do yard work for widows who couldn't help themselves.

Steven loved talking to people and helping whenever he could. To his surprise, he made many new friends who were old enough to be his grandmother. He also learned to love people the way Jesus loved them.

Spending his summer building a lawn-mowing business changed his life in many wonderful ways, and he didn't regret it.

WHY DOES IT MATTER?

Life is full of decisions, and many times the choices aren't necessarily bad versus good. Often, we have multiple good options, with each choice having a positive outcome.

Strangely, these decisions can be the hardest, especially when we're afraid of making the wrong choice or living with regret.

But God doesn't want us to live in fear. He wants us to trust Him and just *do something* that will bring Him glory.

"Trust your work to the Lord, and your plans will work out well" (Proverbs 16:3).